INSIDE OUT

Unlocking God's Treasures Within Our Hearts

PAULA CONNELLY

WestBow
PRESS
A DIVISION OF THOMAS NELSON

WestBow Press books may be ordered through booksellers or by contacting:

WestBow Press
A Division of Thomas Nelson
1663 Liberty Drive
Bloomington, IN 47403
www.westbowpress.com
1-(866) 928-1240

ISBN: 978-1-4497-4977-4 (sc)
ISBN: 978-1-4497-4976-7 (hc)
ISBN: 978-1-4497-4978-1 (e)

Library of Congress Control Number: 2012907622

Printed in the United States of America

WestBow Press rev. date: 12/3/2012

DEDICATION

I would like to dedicate this book to my sister Tracey who has inspired me to never give up in the face of adversity.

To the Lord Jesus Christ my life is dedicated and all praise goes to Him for He is the one who has rescued my heart and set me free!

Now to all who are seeking for a new heart and life from the inside out ~ Jesus is the only way!

'Be strong and courageous'

CONTENTS

Acknowledgments

My thanks and appreciation, go to so many wonderful people and friends who have encouraged me and supported me through the journey of *Inside Out* and the writing of my story. Thank you to Georgina Chong-You for editing, proof reading and helping to pull it altogether and to Anne for hours of time proofreading.

To the prayer warriors for your love and support Anne, Tracey, Wendy Lorraine, Kim, Narelle and Loreen you are incredible! To my dear girlfriends for lots of laughs, tears and just walking out life together, you are all such a blessing.

Thank you to my mentors and friends, Pastors Lilian and Pastor Richard Tng, Pastor Chris and Sally Hope and the support from many in the body of Christ who have inspired my life and the journey of inside out.

Most of all to my darling Husband Graeme who has been a rock through not only the writing of *Inside Out*, but helping me to live this message and being an amazing man of continual grace and strength through it all.

And to our three amazing children, Matt, Amy, Ellie for being so supportive in the time spent writing and for being so beautiful, you are the greatest blessing in my life.

To my family: Mum, Dad, all my amazing sisters and brother for years of encouragement and love. You're the most amazing family anyone could ever hope for. **All Praise and Glory go to Jesus the Lord and Saviour of my life, whom without I am nothing! Thank you.**

Endorsements

I have known Paula for a long time. It has been my privilege to be her Pastor from the day she walked into our church as a 16year old twenty-five years ago and became born again.

Paula, her husband Graeme and their three awesome children are very normal, everyday kind of people who live with such passionate devotion to Christ, church, life, fun, family & friends.

The book that Paula has written has taken a lifetime to write. It is her story of Christ's amazing grace. What she has written is how she does life all day every day. It is not theory, speech and doctrine but her very real journey into strength, freedom and a whole new day of joy and forever peace.

Well done, Paula. May this book reproduce in many a deep desire to live changed lives from the inside out.

Warren McMartin
Senior Pastor/Faith City, Albury/Wodonga (2011)

The Bible teaches us that man looks at the outward appearance, but God looks at the heart. At times we can go through life so busy making sure everything 'looks' all right on the outside. Meanwhile what exactly is it that God sees when He looks at our hearts?

Some of us are so busy we haven't stopped to visit those places in our hearts that tell us who we are. In her book "Inside Out" Paula shares how God took her from being a fearful, angry, controlling woman to a relaxed, faith-filled woman ready for anything that life has for her.

As you read this book you will find illuminations about the state of your own heart that will give you a clearer picture of what God is seeing when He looks at you. Paula shares insights from the Word of God that will transform the state of your heart to be pleasing in God's sight. This is a must read for all women!

Sally Hope
Global freedom Church

This is a book that brings life and testimony to the Word of God. What I like about the content is that Paula did not just share a story or her knowledge of the word, but through her own experience displays the power of the WORD (God Himself) that gives strength and brings restoration. Her testimony proves the WORD that generates faith to replace fear, love to replace insecurity and peace to replace anxiety. All these will bring us into the haven of REST. I believe many women need to read this book because we are or may be going through similar struggles like Paula did. Sadly we can be so busy doing and achieving that we neglect to guard our hearts and eventually end up distressed physically, emotionally, depressed and hopeless. This is not the kind of life God has for us. His plan is that we can live, love and laugh now and in the days to come. Indeed a great book that will unlock the beauty of every woman's heart.

Pastor Lilian Tng
International Rock Church and GEMS ministry

"The Kingdom of God is like hidden treasure waiting to be found. You must seek it out. It's like a precious pearl hidden in a field."

INTRODUCTION

Isaiah 61 Jesus has come to heal the broken hearted
and set the captives free!

No matter what the condition of your life or heart, these words are true for today. Jesus has come to heal the broken hearted, to open prison doors and to release captives. This book is about that very thing happening to me and what's more it's for everyone. No matter what age or stage of life you may be at or what circumstances you may be dealing with today, Jesus has come to give us life abundantly from the inside out. In every area of our lives - body, soul and spirit.

It all starts with our hearts . . .

*   *   *

How is your heart going? Mine was not in good shape several years ago upon which my journey took me to searching for answers, underneath my skin. We can spend so much time fixing up the external of our lives and making them look good! But this time I was forced to go deeper. No amount of makeovers or plastic surgery could fix this, my heart was in trouble and I needed an internal makeover! (Though I wouldn't mind a nip and tuck in some places!).

What I discovered led me to a realisation of the importance of working on our lives from the inside out and by doing this, real transformation takes place in our hearts, minds and in what we believe. Thus the changes I so desired have come about. As we journey through the pages of this book, I pray it will speak to your heart and bring a message of light into darkness and hope for all hearts. It's a continual journey but a good one as we learn to surrender our hearts to God on a daily basis. Our destination: to fall into the arms of love and grace, healing and comfort, and freedom from all our fears!

We can go to doctors and have regular physical body and heart checks, which is important, but we also need to be mindful of our own spiritual healthy heart checks, (sometimes we can be too afraid to admit what's going on inside our hearts).

The heart how precious a thing it is. Without it we cannot live, within it contains our deepest desires, hopes and dreams. **The Bible says eternity is set in our hearts (Ecclesiastes 3:11).** Just like our physical heart pumps life flowing into every part of our body, so it is with our spiritual heart within us. If there is anything blocking or clogging up our valves we can be in serious trouble, it can stop the flow of life from the way it should be. How can we ignore this vital organ's health, when it contains life!

Yet as I have personally discovered, we can ignore it. We can bury things within the chambers of our heart until it's so clogged with painful memories, hurts or fear let alone the present challenges we may be facing. No

The heart is the spiritual hub of the home.

matter what is happening right now in your life, God cares about your heart and it's in His promises for us to know the Truth. The Truth will make us free (John 8:31-32)—freedom from all worry or anxiety, free from confusion or past hurts . . . simply free.

Life can throw things at us we are just not prepared for and only then the truth of what's been hidden comes to the surface. This was the case for me and my journey of healing in my heart.

In Proverbs 4:23 there are three powerful words **above all else** . . .

As I have pondered the importance of these words, a message of life and truth has evolved within my own heart—a truth I pray will open eyes and hearts to understanding and transformation.

'Above all else, guard your heart for it is the wellspring of life.' (New International version)

Let me say that again, it is the wellspring of life! The Amplified Bible says, 'for out of it flow the springs of life.'

Above all else we are advised to guard our hearts. Above all the important things we can do in life, this is a key to living life in abundance. (John 10:10) What does it mean to guard our hearts? Is it about putting up walls within our hearts that will protect from the issues that arise? (We will discuss this further in the chapters).

Obviously, this means our hearts are very important to God and further to this, Jesus has come to make His home in our hearts, what good news! (Ephesians 3:17) We are not on our own; He has given us everything we need to live a full life inside out.

Our hearts act like containers in the very centre of our being, catching everything that enters, like a storehouse. I liken it to the kitchen in our home where all the goodies are stored then filtered out and everyone gets fed. **The heart is the spiritual hub of the home.** We are the home and the heart is the source of all things.

The heart is the wellspring of life from where things flow. It is the source, the beginning of where life flows. Like a water spring is the source of where water comes from, were it to be poisoned it would flow into all the rivers and then everything would be polluted. How much more should we keep and guard our hearts, the source of life! What we filter life through is our hearts. Much can be hidden in our hearts, good or bad, positive or negative, truth or lies. The heart is revealed through life's challenges, crisis times and daily life, even by what we speak as in Luke 6:45b *'for out of the abundance (overflow) of the heart his mouth speaks.*

The question is what is coming out of the abundance—overflow—of our hearts? Is it the fullness of life, love, peace and joy? Or is it the overflow of our hurts, fears, worries and anxiety about our life?

From the inside out—
Internal verses External

In a world where many are pursuing extreme *external* makeovers in an attempt to find satisfaction, inner peace and happiness, *Inside Out* reveals truths about finding true

> *"Above all else . . . guard your heart."*

and genuine treasure inside the heart that will last a lifetime. These truths will not only transform your outer life but most importantly, your inner life—the inner you, which is the hidden person of the heart. You will find true peace, love, joy and healing from the inside out.

No doctors or operations will transform you, but only cooperation and a willingness to allow the Master Surgeon, God Himself, to dig deep into the inner chambers of the heart. Therefore, unlocking any past hurts, lies of the enemy, disappointments or fears and replacing them with God's promises and the treasures contained in His Word will bring life and healing.

Through a time of brokenness and ill health I found these treasures and discovered the healing power of Jesus. Though the journey took some time and a process of continually learning new ways, what I discovered far

> *God has come to give us a new heart, new mind, new life and healing from the inside out.*

outweighed the sickness that tried to bind me. Deep within my heart were the real issues that eventually became the reason for the physical illness that befell me, hence the title *Inside Out*.

What is truly important is for us to look after not only the external, but the internal health of our lives. Becoming a whole person, body, soul and spirit is about paying proper attention to all these three areas of our life.

We can fix up the external but it doesn't fix the internal. We can look great on the outside but be rotten on the inside. When we don't work from the inside out we only keep coming back to the same place of wanting more of something that doesn't satisfy, or going around the same mountain of frustration in our lives. It's only when we search deeper into the heart like David the Psalmist said, 'Search my heart o God,' that we find what we are looking for. **God has come to give us a new heart, new mind, new life and healing from the inside out.**

Jesus has made a way for us to live strong, overcoming, faith filled lives through keeping and guarding our hearts in His word. No one is exempt from coming under pressure or trials in this world, but its how we get through them that will determine whether *we become better or bitter as a result.*

> *How do you keep and guard your heart?*
> *How do you find strength to go on in difficult times?*

These are some of the questions I will try my best to answer through the testimony of my own personal time of crisis and subsequent healing. But even more importantly, I want to tell of how God showed me His treasures in living out of His transforming Word that brought the life and healing from the inside out.

I was healed physically, emotionally and strengthened as a result of finding these treasures. My life is better now as a result of going through this dark valley and I am grateful for knowing what I now know. Trials are never easy at the time, they are painful and tormenting and hard to bear. However, they reveal our need for someone greater than ourselves—**our Saviour Jesus.**

How amazing it can be that through our trials we find the richest treasures of all. Paul the apostle said it like this in James 1:2:

"Consider it wholly joyful, my brethren whenever you are enveloped in or encounter trials of any sort or fall into various temptations. Be assured and understand that the trial and proving of your faith bring out endurance and steadfastness and patience. But let endurance and steadfastness and patience have full play and do a thorough work, so that you may be (people) perfectly and fully developed (with no defects) lacking in nothing."

As believers we are called to believe and put our confidence and trust in the Lord Jesus Christ. Through Him being at work in our lives we overcome the world and its trials. Many believers are not living in their full authority in the Word of God. I know because I too was like this. However we are called to be the head and not the tail, above and not beneath. It is time for us to arise and live in the fullness of His power at work in our lives. It's time to activate the promises of God's riches from His word for the inside of our hearts.

Through the pages of this book, it's my desire that you find what I have found: life-giving promises and a new heart. God is still healing, restoring, saving and re-building people's lives all over the planet; my hope is that you find Him and the treasures that are in His Word for your heart today.

I have told you these things, so that in Me you may have perfect peace and confidence. In the world you have tribulation and trials and distress and frustration; but be of good cheer (take courage; be confident, certain, undaunted)! For I have overcome the world.

(I have deprived it of power to harm you and have conquered it for you.

—*John 16:33*

MY STORY

It was the year 2000 a new millennium and my world as I knew it was about to take a life-altering turn. Suddenly it can happen, a crisis or trial that seems to make its way into our world in an attempt to knock us right off our feet. My world was about to come to a halt, not exactly what I had in mind for a new year.

I was busy with building our new home and doing many things being a wife and mother of three, working in our business and in our church as the Worship Pastor. Life was pretty full. On the outside I was doing what I knew to do, but inside I didn't have a real peace, my heart was troubled.

I had not been well for a few months and physically things had started to get on top of me. I had been pushing through for a while, thinking *'I will get through this'*. But the fatigue was fighting my body and mind; I simply didn't have the time to stop long enough to address it. This is when the unexpected happened; something I had not planned entered my usually controlled and organised life.

It was like the rug had been pulled from underneath me and I couldn't go on, just getting out of bed became a problem. I felt this continual heaviness over my mind and body, like carrying a heavy weight.

Eventually my body gave way with exhaustion and I couldn't physically go on.

With my head spinning from dizziness, there was not much more I could do, but lie there and hope it passed. This is how I started to wake up daily and retire daily, morning and night with fear as my guide and heaviness over my mind. Fear was plaguing me to say the least. Fear of ill health, fear of the future, and anxiety were rampant in my heart. The night times seemed to be the worst. Shaking uncontrollably for hours at night, with what seemed like fevers (but later diagnosed as adrenaline rushes, seemingly highs and lows in my blood sugar), all caused from too much stress going on the inside of me. I couldn't switch my mind off; I desperately needed some answers as to why this was happening.

I knew it was there, all along, this sense of fear and dread. Finally it took its toll on my physical health. I can't help but wonder how many people are experiencing stress and anxiety like this right now and just pushing through, without any idea of where it could be headed. The realisation of how stress affects the body, both physically and emotionally is imperative in becoming a healthy and whole person.

I was living in the fast lane, one day rolling into another, under girded with a continual nagging of fear, stress and anxiety. For many months my family, friends and pastor were telling me to slow down and stop striving. To be honest I thought they were crazy, I wasn't going to let this thing beat me, but beat me it did because I was insistent on running in my own strength and not in God's strength. I ignored all the warning signs within my own heart for several months.

We can be driven for all the wrong or right reasons in life and I had some good ones (and some not so good). I was driven, but driven by fear. Fear of the future, fear of not achieving, and fear of missing the mark, on top of fearing for my family and the things I thought were normal to fear about. All of my dreams and hopes for the future had to be put on the shelf; it became just one day at a time, one step in front of the other, because that's all I could manage with the fatigue and exhaustion.

It's amazing how our thoughts can rule us and seemingly make us believe they are true, this is where fear got the better of me. From the outside I may have looked strong and my world looked complete as though I had everything in hand, (we can be very good at masking our problems). However, on the inside I was in turmoil in my heart and mind, I desperately wanted to be free from the torment of fear that had been plaguing me.

I cried out to God. He has a way of allowing us to come to the end of ourselves. What I mean is I was running in my own strength and not in His. I was not living in His grace, but constantly striving in my own ways to make things happen. I had to get to the end of me, and my way of living and doing things. By nature I am a go-getter, never give up, get over it girl, but I had to learn that striving in my own strength was not effective, and I have since learned this lesson.

I want to make it clear, God doesn't cause sickness or put fear on us. I know that for certain because there is an enemy, satan being the father of all lies and who comes to kill steal and destroy (John 10:10). God didn't put this sickness on me to prove a point. It's not His nature; He is our healer, our refuge and our strength. He is the God and Father of all hope, comfort and love.

The truth is **I had not dealt with the fears deep in my heart** for many years and it was time to allow them to come to the surface so they could be swept away forever. God knew I was about to go through this dark valley and He was with me through it all.

At the beginning of my journey of healing Proverbs 4:23 was a key scripture and life saving word for me. God heard my prayer!

> *Proverbs 4:23 tells us to "keep and guard our hearts with all vigilance and above all that you guard, for out of it flow the springs (issues) of life."*

How fear was born

The heart is the centre of who we are, likened to the hub or the core of our being, where everything is derived. The Bible says 'above all else' keep and guard our hearts. The heart here is described as the wellspring meaning the source or beginning from where life flows. This is why it is so important for us to keep and guard our hearts. But God is in the healing business and this Scripture was a direct key to me discovering the root of my problem with fear and to finding healing.

Fear found its way into my heart as a child. I had grown up in fear and well into adulthood the same fears were plaguing me. My parents raised me in the Catholic Church; however I did not have a personal relationship with Jesus as my Lord and Saviour. I had mostly pictured God out of fear of punishment and judgement than out of love and grace. My view of God was distorted to say the least. I viewed God as though He was angry at me for my wrongs, therefore I had no real concept of Him loving me or carrying my burdens. It wasn't until I encountered Christ at 18 years of age where I was born again and found my personal relationship with Him that these misconceptions began to unfold. However, I still needed to learn and understand how to live out of the fullness of His grace and love in my life, this was part of my journey of finding the truth and learning to trust God whole heartedly with my life. Trust being the key word here!

During my childhood years there was a lot of strife in our family. Ongoing financial pressures and raising six children created difficult times for my parents. There was a lot of fighting and not much peace in our home. Sometimes this would go on for days and weeks, even months at a time, which didn't make for a secure peace-filled home. There were times when my parents threatened divorce or separation, which left us feeling unstable, insecure and not knowing what was ahead. I realise now that this was when the fear began in my heart—I was afraid of our family breaking up or something bad happening to us. I know my parents loved me but somehow dread was always in the back of my mind.

More than anything fear became something I knew on a daily basis as normal and I learnt to cope with it (believing its lies). Somehow this seemed to be my safety net, as I put up my own walls to hide behind for security. I became my own protector, which means I was in control. These walls of fear built one brick at a time through many other of life's challenges became the very thing that trapped me in a lifestyle of fear and dread deep within my own heart; like being imprisoned from the inside out.

Until truth is revealed you don't know how else to live and this was the case for me. I learnt a pattern of self-protection and control and as long as I could control what happened then I felt safe. This was a fulltime job that led to the sickness of chronic fatigue, exhaustion and stress, accompanied by stomach problems and pain throughout most of the day.

I am fortunate to say the Lord has been faithful to my family. Today we are a whole new family, not only has God personally healed me but my parent's marriage. Today they have been married for 54 years and as a result of their faithfulness many have been saved. Theirs is a wonderful testimony of the Lord's healing power in their marriage. My husband Graeme and I have been married 25 years and still going strong. It's true that through the trials we encounter we can learn a better way, as we put our hand in God's hand, He reveals the way through the darkest times into His light.

Before I go on, I want to assure you that Jesus is the same today, yesterday and forever, He is our Healer, and His Word is Truth. Through my time of illness He came to my rescue, and He never left my side. He healed me inside and out and revealed treasures I never knew prior to this journey. He surely shines in the darkest times of our life and will renew us. Jesus is the only way to a new heart and a complete life.

My prayer is that He will do the same for you, hold you in the night hours, be your guide to a better day and bring complete healing and treasures into your life—treasures you never knew were possible or even there to be grasped. I have put scriptures throughout this book for you to think, meditate and rebuild your life upon.

This is my story and testimony of healing from the inside out. The Lord showed me His grace and favour and has brought me into a whole new way of living with a physically, emotionally, and spiritually restored heart. It is only through a real living relationship with the Lord Jesus Christ that our hearts are truly fully transformed and healed, all glory be to Him.

As we journey through these pages together, let the Living Word of God reignite your heart, bring light into the dark places, unfolding new revelation and insight in the knowledge of Him and most of all build new treasures of *truth* inside your heart. Consider this a treasure hunt for your heart and as you ask the Holy Spirit He will lead you into all truth just as He did for me.

INSIDE OUT

*As far as the heavens reach to you my hearts crying out, as far as the
ocean cover the earth my eyes search for you.
As long as there's breath in me there is life
As long as there's hope there is faith*

**You're healing me from the inside out
You're healing me and I won't doubt
You're healing me . . .**

*I'm not trapped inside of fear, I've taken my heart from this doubt I
won't stay here in this place you're healing me inside and out
As long as there's breath in me there is life
As long as there's hope there is faith*

*When I think of all you've done, your arms outstretched for me.
By your wounds I am healed I have forgiveness that sets me free,
You're healing me from the inside out*

©Paula Connelly 2005 Instrumental album Inside Out

"For God who said let light shine out of darkness, has shone in our hearts so as (to beam forth) the Light for the illumination of the knowledge of the majesty and glory of God (as it is manifest in the Person and is revealed) in the face of Jesus Christ (the Messiah).

However we possess this precious treasure (the divine light of the Gospel) in (frail, human) vessels of earth that the grandeur and exceeding greatness of the power may be shown to be from God and not from ourselves."

—2 Corinthians 4:6, 7

"It's the heart that matters and matters of the heart need to be uncovered and rediscovered."

CHAPTER ONE

UNLOCKING THE TREASURE CHEST

~Reflection~

*I*t was a cool Monday evening, and I had just come back from a bike ride with my husband, up and down the hills watching the sun go down for the evening. It was exhilarating and inspirational. As I was riding with the cool air against my face and the breeze in my hair, welling up deep within my heart was a sense of freedom and laughter.

I couldn't help but reflect upon the last eight years of my life. I've gained a freedom to think for myself, my health and strength have returned to me, I am now healed from all the years of anxiety, fear and stress that once ravaged my body so terribly, and now I am freer than ever on the inside. I can look back and honestly thank God for bringing me through that season of my life.

The lessons I have learned and the joy that has come from it overwhelm my heart. Hindsight is interesting, but the truth is **it's the trials we go through that really make us who we are.**

Like a child riding without a care in the world, all I could do was laugh and think how good God is, He restored my life. You see a few years ago I couldn't even contemplate getting on a bike; just the thought of it was exhausting. This is why riding a bike now is so much joy. I count each day a wonderful blessing to have my health and be able to do the smallest things in life.

Losing your health is very debilitating just as is losing your hope or joy and love for life. Sadly many are in these situations. The good news is that Jesus came to restore life to us, freedom from all our fears, freedom to live life to the fullest. This is what inside out living is all about and to get there we have some **treasure hunting** to do.

> **Matthew 6:21 "For where your treasure is there your heart will be also."**

Are you looking for treasure beyond this world? Happiness, peace, a stress-free life? Certainly all of us would like this and more. A life of abundance and overflowing from the inside out is what Jesus Christ came to offer us. It's free, and it's for a lifetime—for eternity.

We can search all of our lives to be fulfilled by this world's system and materialistic lifestyle, but only end up dissatisfied with the quality of our lives; always striving for more but never getting enough. I have discovered that *what the world has to offer doesn't last, but what the Word of God has to offer is everlasting.*

> **Ecclesiastes 3:11 "He has made everything beautiful in its time. Also He has put eternity in their hearts . . . that deep sense and longing for more beyond this world."**

In order to discover the more, we need to go deeper beyond the surface. Like a diver looking for treasures on the bottom of the ocean; we need to search our hearts.

David the Psalmist sums it up in Psalm 139:23-24 where he says, *"Search me, O God and know my heart; Try me and know my anxieties; And see if there is any wicked way in me, and lead me in the way everlasting."*

It's the trials we go through that really make us who we are.

When we take these words to heart and seriously allow God to search our hearts unafraid of what we may find, we allow Him by His love and grace into the secret places to begin working in and through us.

As I have done this what I discovered has changed my life and brought me healing and wholeness from the inside out.

It starts with surrendering our lives to Him. In an act of faith as we pray this same prayer David prayed, God begins unlocking the hurts, the past, the hidden fears and the process of healing begins.

We must begin to dethrone self and enthrone the God of all grace to enter into our hearts. A life that is complete and a sound peaceful mind is something we all desire and strive for. In Christ there is no striving but through His grace and ability He empowers us to live this life to the fullest and to overcome obstacles along the way.

Unlocking any negative, lifeless traits within our hearts is the key and replacing them with the treasures found in God's word is what completely renews our minds and hearts. These are obtainable for every one of us on a daily basis.

Look to your heart
There is so much to be realized about the heart. The heart is like a container of life. Our personalities, thoughts, ideas about our life and who we are, motivations, and desire for certain things in our life all stem from our hearts desires. We are all so uniquely and individually designed but God looks upon the heart of man, that's the real person underneath our skin.

> *We can chase after the world's treasures or we can pursue the treasures that truly satisfy the heart.*

The heart contains the real person. Locked away are all those untapped dreams, hopes and desires yet to be realized. In the very centre and core of our being these exist, along with our values, convictions and beliefs about our life. Our hearts also contend with our doubts, fears and negative attitudes, along with our deepest longings for love and acceptance.

Like a coin there are two sides to it, just as in life there is the good and the bad, the positive and the negative, the heart it seems can contain both sides of the coin. There may be times we function out of the truth we know in our hearts and other times, negative thoughts and imaginations can try to influence us in our thinking.

The question is; *What thoughts do we allow to rule in our hearts and minds?*

What thoughts occupy the throne of our hearts? Stop! Take a moment to think about the things that are ruling your heart.

Consider the attitudes and motives of the heart, both healthy and unhealthy that can live within us at times. We need to carefully examine our motivations. (As I have mentioned, striving was one of my unhealthy heart issues, I didn't recognize for a long time until I was burnt out from all the stress.)

With the pressures and stresses of life, it's becoming more apparent that people desire a more prosperous and peaceful life or an easier way to do life, (though oftentimes it gets complicated). The simplicity of true peace and prosperity comes from knowing Gods word and His will for our hearts.

Things get complicated when we have too much going on the inside of us and no clear priorities. *Anxiety in the heart weighs a man down.*

The Bible says in Luke 6:45: 'Out of the abundance (overflow) of the heart his mouth speaks' and in Proverbs 23:7: 'As a man thinks in his heart so is he'.

No one knows or sees into the heart like God.

So, who are we in our hearts? What is going on the inside of us? What comes out of us is a direct result of the inside of our lives and what's going into it. If there is peace within, then peace flows out, or if there is anxiety in the heart, then stress will flow out.

If we want to live out our dreams and desires or to discover true happiness and peace on the inside of our lives, we must first look to the heart of things. It's amazing what you will find, when you search your heart.

> *Proverbs 17:22 "A happy heart is good medicine and a cheerful mind works healing, but a broken spirit dries up the bones."*

Searching for true happiness and peace

In my own journey from illness to health and healing I discovered much more than I imagined. But it was within my heart I made the most amazing discoveries. Coming from brokenness and fear to finding strength and peace in Christ deep within my heart and being forever changed as a result, my life is better for going through this crisis time.

In the search for true peace and happiness (that is joy and contentment) we must be willing to look deeper into the chambers of our hearts. When we look only for happiness within our external or material surroundings, we are left with a dissatisfaction on the inside. There may be temporary satisfaction, but soon or later we find ourselves saying, *"there's got to be more to life?"*

Oftentimes we can carry the weight of the world on our shoulders or disappointments and broken dreams on the inside of us, which was the case for me during this time, leaving me with a broken heart.

'Hope deferred makes the heart sick, but when the desire is fulfilled it is a tree of life".(Proverbs 13:12)

As a result of the many pressures and stresses in today's lifestyle, anxiety, depression and other mental, emotional illnesses are increasing, leaving many feeling hopeless about their lives and future.

What we allow to develop in us through the trials of life, will either bring out the best or the worst, making us better or bitter.

As we keep our eyes fixed on Jesus, He brings the Joy and peace we need. The Bible says, Jesus came to set all who are oppressed of the devil free. (Acts 10:38)

This includes freedom from the weights and burdens of this world. In exchange, we receive the promises of God; His life of abundance in our hearts, overflowing with goodness. Like a fountain of joy welling up and flowing out of our hearts and it's available to us every day.

> *John 10:10 Jesus said, "I came that they may have and enjoy life, and have it in abundance (to the full, till it overflows)."*

As I have discovered this complete satisfaction and peace is found in no other but Christ. Through abiding in His Love, His peace, and Joy, we begin to experience our lives on a whole new level of wellbeing and completeness in Him from the inside out. Along with a renewed perspective and ability that enables us to do all things in and through His strength and grace.

Renovate your life from the Inside Out

Are you wanting a new you? I have seen so many TV shows on makeovers and renovating guides to a new life externally and even in material wealth, it all seems so wonderful, but the truth is, you can fix up the outside and still have all the problems on the inside. It would be like fixing up the outside of a home and walking in only to find the inside left with its old cracked walls, paint peeling, stained carpets and old damp smell. Immediately you forget the outside appearance. The atmosphere of the home comes from within. It makes no real difference if the outside looks fantastic it's the inside you have to live in.

A few years ago we visited New York City and I can remember entering the hotel foyer it was so beautiful and extravagant. However, when we entered the lift to the rooms, we noticed a huge dip in the floor of the hallways to our room. We opened the door of our room and could not believe how small and how run down it was. We were totally taken aback and disappointed because the foyer had been so beautiful, but the inner rooms were the complete opposite.

We don't want our lives to be like this; we have to live with ourselves and like who we are inside and out. I'm here to tell you Jesus can heal your heart, make you new and give you a whole new life so that you *can* like who you are. I have heard it said home is where the heart is!

God the Builder

God promises a new life through Jesus Christ!	

It's interesting that Jesus came as a carpenter? He not only knew how to build houses, but lives. God is the builder of our lives. Re-building our dreams, hopes and giving us purpose and meaning in life. I am married to a builder so over the years I have come to understand a bit about building a home or renovating a house. If you want a new home you must have a plan, a vision of that new home design. If you want to renovate your home, you must also have a plan of what you want it to look like. A vision is seeing it in your heart first. Although your new home is not built yet, you can see it and imagine what it will be like when it is built.

But this is where God comes in. He has a plan for everyone's life. It's new and complete. I love that word, NEW! It gives the impression of a new start, new beginning, everything fresh and shiny. God comes to light up our path and give us His plan and direction for our lives. It's a plan for good and not for evil. We need to see this plan for our life through His eyes. He is the builder and we are the home He is building. Moreover, our hearts are the centres of the home.

Our bodies are the houses and our hearts are what I call the hub of the home, where the important things happen. It's like the kitchen, the place where food is prepared to be eaten, and the substance that keeps us going. Just as our bodies need physical food our hearts need spiritual food to keep us healthy spiritually, emotionally and mentally.

To renovate the inside of our lives we must be willing to open the door of our hearts and allow Jesus in. Let God get right in there and do something about the old hurts we hold in our hearts. It's time to toss out the old and put in the new. He has come to make us new creations! In fact, 1 Corinthians 6:19 says our bodies are the temple of the Holy Spirit.

When God comes to take up residence He lights up the whole of our temple, giving us a new heart, new mind and a new life. It's called being born again (John 3:16).

But we still must decide daily to live our lives according to the Word of God and the truth it contains, as we are led by our newly born again spirit. Now that our hearts are awakened to this new life we don't become robots set on automatic, we must learn to be guided and led by the Holy Spirit and cooperate with Him daily.

Replace the old with the new

The key to renovating your life from the inside out is in replacing the old with the new. Living out of the new person we are in Christ and being renewed in our hearts and minds. As we allow the Holy Spirit access into our hearts and minds He leads us in creating new thought patterns and ways of living. As we yield our whole person to Him, he renews our personalities into His likeness and nature. This must be a daily process of being renewed in the Word of God as we put His truth into our hearts and minds. Practically speaking, you've got to read God's Word everyday and be filled with His Spirit in order to get His Truth in your heart and mind.

Sometimes we can leave unresolved hurts, wounds, fears, disappointments, or un-forgiveness deep in our hearts, which blocks the way to living completely free from the past or the old ways of living and reacting.

Certain situations can trigger our emotions, bringing up things from the past and leaving us feeling guilty, unworthy or ashamed.

As we remember Jesus is always in us and He will never leave us, He continues His work in us and He will complete what He started, that is in perfecting Himself in us.

> *Philippians 1:6 "And I am convinced and sure of the very thing, that He who begun a good work in you will continue until the day of Jesus Christ, (right up to the time of His return), developing (that good work) and perfecting and bring it to full completion in you."*

If lying deep within our hearts are unresolved hurts and issues, they only produce unhealthy patterns of living, (in our thoughts and emotions). These can be destructive when left for years untouched and unhealed, becoming hindrances to our faith and stopping our hearts from being completely free.

The torment they bring to our hearts becomes a barrier to living a victorious Christian life. I have seen this in my own life and many others. They need to be washed away, renewed and replaced with the promises of God for our lives. This is why I am emphasizing that we renew and renovate our lives from the inside out.

It begins with our hearts!

"And the light shines on in the darkness, for the darkness has never overpowered it." John 1:5

CHAPTER TWO

UNCOVER MY HEART

~My Journey~

So there I was, looking for the light amidst this dark place in my life, desperately needing some answers. The best way I could describe it was like being in a dark pit, or going through a long dark tunnel with no light at the end, not even a glimpse. With the fatigue weighing my body down and my mind in a constant fog of dizziness, I laid in my bed contemplating how I would get through the day. Darkness has a way of creating fear, fear of the unknown and fear of the future.

I questioned whether the light was going to shine? Although I knew the Light was Jesus, it all seemed so confusing and I couldn't see through this darkness; something was blocking the way. Dragging myself out of bed was a major effort, each night was filled with restlessness and insomnia and I felt as though I could sleep all day.

The normal routine of getting the children off to school in the mornings became quite an ordeal, leaving me feeling so exhausted and dizzy. I was not very stable on my feet, which was all so frustrating and I was much slower than normal. I found it difficult attending to the smallest of demands because it all took so much more effort.

My husband was a tremendous help, he did almost everything, including all the running around after school, grocery shopping, as well as running our business and attending to all of its demands. Not to mention we were right in the middle of building our new home, which was a huge demand on both of us. God gave him an incredible capacity during this time for us both. I am still amazed today how we got through.

I love that verse in Ecclesiastes that says two are better than one, when one is down, the other one can help him up (Ecclesiastes 4:9,10). There was so much to do and one of the hardest things as a mother and wife is not being well enough to be there for your own family. I wanted so much for this to end and to return to normal.

Burnt out and stressed
Being burnt out from all the stress, pressure and living in the fast lane for so long had brought me to this place: not paying attention to the issues of my heart or my physical health, like a fuse burnt out of its socket. My body was letting me know it couldn't go on this way. My strength was next to none, my mind was overly anxious and my heart burdened, I was fearful of the future and each day had too many cares of its own to deal with.

All the striving in my own strength and pushing way beyond normal limits had cost me my health. At this time I had to lay down my position as worship pastor at our church, my work in the business and all my hopes and dreams were put on the shelf. The weight of letting everyone down was also something I found difficult to deal with. I wasn't exactly helping anyone, but I had to let go and let God take control.

GOD had a plan!
I am great believer in things happening for a reason, there is a purpose to everything under the sun. I knew God would not have allowed all of this to happen to me if He didn't have a plan behind it all. My hope was that I would find out what that might be. Although I was the one who led me into this by pushing myself too hard all the time, there had been warning signs in my health, which I had paid no attention to.

> *Jeremiah 29:11 "For I know the thoughts and plans that I have for you, says the Lord, thoughts and plans for welfare and peace and not for evil to give you hope in your final outcome."*

I had read the words of Jeremiah 29:11 so often and I was holding onto these precious words as my life support for each day and their eventual outcome.

The situation didn't change over-night, however, it was one day at a time, one step at a time. I was learning patience very quickly, which was something I hadn't been very good at before. I tend to be a very driven person by nature and a leader who likes things done right away, so to be sitting around doing nothing and waiting was very out of character for me. For the first time in my life, I was out of control!

The Key to Unlocking treasures is in Prayer

With so many questions unanswered there was only one thing to do, so I prayed. With my Bible as the map and the Holy Spirit as my guide I was determined to get to the bottom of this. Although the doctors did many tests, they didn't offer me many solutions. They offered me anti-depressants for the stress (which I declined) and then told me to go home and rest. I was hoping for a different solution or a quick fix to my problem. Their best solution was likened to putting a band-aid over my wound. I know they meant well, but deep down I had to do some soul searching of my own. **This is where my journey of inside out began.**

Crying out for a Word from God, my prayers were soon to be answered but not quite as I had in mind.

> *Isaiah 59:1 says, "Behold the Lord's hand is not shortened at all, that it cannot save, nor His ear dull with deafness that it cannot hear."*

He hears our cries for help, even though at times it may seem that He doesn't hear because our answers come so slowly, or we don't get the answer we were hoping for. None the less He is there, even in the silence. Faith is placing our complete dependence and trust in Him in these difficult times.

I remember standing in an altar call one particular night at our church. There I was waiting in line to receive prayer (as often people would at the end of the service), along came the guest preacher who had been speaking that night and as he went to place his hand on me to pray, he yelled, "She's stressed!"

There was my Word from God! It didn't seem very spiritual, but it was what the doctors had also told me. He also advised me to take time off and rest. My biggest problem was working out how I was going to take all this time off, but he got my attention and I knew I had to surrender and just do it. More than anything, it was the rest in my heart from all the worry and striving that I needed. God was answering my prayer; I just didn't understand all of it at this point.

For six months only my husband knew how ill I was, holding me in the night hours as my body shook and trembled from all the anxiety that had taken over my heart. I had hidden my problem as best as I could, after all I didn't want people to think I didn't have it all together.

I now realise that was part of my problem. For some reason as leaders we think we have to have everything perfect in our lives. Jesus is the one perfect person and the truth is we are first children of God—His sons and daughters saved by grace not by works. Secondly we need to be honest with ourselves and about what's going on in our lives. We are all a work in progress, with Christ perfecting Himself in us as we cooperate with Him every day of our lives. Being vulnerable can seem hard for a leader. We must be willing to be open and honest and say in those difficult times, "I haven't got it all together, but I am trusting in Jesus to help me."

I have since learnt this important lesson of accountability and just being the best me I can be with God's help even if I don't have everything perfectly in its place. God loves me and together we will work out the rest. I have certainly come a long way from where I was. By allowing ourselves to be honest and accountable to someone like our spouse, or a trusted pastor, leader or good friend is the way to keep our lives from pride and helps us to stay on a healthy pathway.

When I realised the truth of my condition, it was the first glimpse of light. I did need to enter rest in my heart and re-evaluate my life. I had to give it all over to the One who is greater—Jesus. It was time to get to the core issues of all my stress and burn out and clear out the blockages to my faith.

Deep into the chambers of the heart
I began soul searching and discovered that deep in my heart were the real issues. It was that part of me that no one else gets to know—only God. It was time to get vulnerable before God, like an open book, the pages of my heart ready to be read one by one, in search for the answers.

No matter what we are trying to mask, until we are willing to go deeper nothing will change. On the outside I had portrayed a person of confidence and that everything was just fine, but inside I was troubled.

I had no peace. I used to think if only I could get away from everything, all the hustle and bustle and rushing around, I would have peace. I was beginning to realise that as long as internally I was not at peace, the turmoil only came with me wherever I went.

> *John14:1 Jesus is with his disciples. He says to them, "let not your hearts be troubled."*

My heart had been troubled for a while, internally things weren't right. On the inside I continually felt anxious and worried about my life. I was desperate for true peace within my heart and for this to happen I needed to allow the master surgeon God and the Holy Spirit deeper into the chambers of my heart.

Sometimes amidst the trials we encounter, we can wonder where God is. At first I felt this way, but as I began to quieten my heart I was able to sense His presence with me. I was beginning to understand that God wasn't in a hurry, not like we are. The physical rest was important and there was a bigger picture I needed to see, the bigger plan that God had in all of this. I was being awakened to new things and His light was beginning to shine in my heart.

Getting to the core of things
I would like to say it happened overnight but my journey of healing was a day-by-day process, things took longer than I expected but God was revealing Himself through His Word to me in so many new ways. Each day unfolded many new treasures from the Word of God. Things I had

not seen before, probably because I didn't take the time to see them. The old saying of taking time to smell the roses comes to my mind. I was smelling the roses for the first time in a long time.

I discovered that I had to be willing to go beyond the surface to get to the core of the issues. Unless we get to the core of the issue, it will lie deep and unresolved. Imagine with me an apple. In the centre of that apple are the seeds. These seeds planted make more apples. It's like that in our hearts, what has been sown over the years makes us who we are. Sometimes if bad seeds are sown—fear, un-forgiveness, or negativity—it causes us to bear bad fruit. We must replant in our hearts the new seeds of love, peace and Gods healing, and then allow these seeds of the Word to grow on the inside of our hearts.

The root cause for me had been years of living in fear. It was time to pull up this weed that had been choking my life.

The Parable of the Sower (Matt 13:18-23)

Sowing the Word of God into our hearts produces faith in our lives. In order to protect those seeds we must remain in the Word of God and abide in His love, otherwise the enemy can come and steal what was sown within our hearts. By allowing the cares of the world, stresses, worries and fear to be all we think on, the seeds of faith are snatched away and we become weak in our believing, unbelief takes root instead. However if we maintain the soil (which is our hearts) guarding against the enemies lies, by living in the Truth the seeds of faith will take root and produce a harvest of fruit in our lives.

There is often a root cause behind sickness and it's the root we need to get to. I am not a great gardener, but I understand that if you don't attend to the plants by tending the soil, watering the plants, nurturing them, digging, and pulling up the weeds, it will get overcrowded, choked by the weeds, and die. I have had this happen in my own garden. It's important when planting any plant that you loosen the roots so they can grow deep into the soil. You have to prepare the soil for the plant to grow.

This was a time of preparation for me and a refining of my roots and foundations in my walk with Jesus, so I could grow even more in faith and into the person He was calling me to be. He was doing some digging in my heart and I had a few weeds that needed to be pulled out! (Matthew 13:22).

> *Unless we get to the core of the issue, it will lie deep and unresolved.*

Seeds of fear had been sown in my life as a child and now they had grown into weeds. These weeds of fear tormented me about my family and my future, always threatening that something bad would happen. I spent most of my years growing up thinking I had to protect myself from being hurt.

Until we are willing to face our fears we will just keep going around the same mountain. I would try not to think about it, but eventually I would just come back to the same place, the fear had become a stronghold and was deeply rooted, it needed to be pulled up roots and all.

Along with the fear I was incredibly insecure. This came from fear growing up, as I said earlier, that my parents would divorce or one of them would leave, and so this sense of abandonment fuelled the fear that was deeply rooted in my heart and the insecurity I felt.

Uncovering the truth about my heart

Upon coming to terms with the truth about my heart I knew I needed to uncover the lies and deceptions the enemy had put in my heart once and for all. I was not going to go on living like this for the rest of my life. I needed to tell someone and get the help I needed to break free of it. Like any lie; once it's uncovered and out, there is a sense of relief. This lie of fear hidden in darkness was about to be exposed to the light and the truth! Sharing our problems with someone else can be half the battle (fear of what others might think), but as we do, we allow it to be brought into the light.

The reality is I didn't get free overnight. I had to begin to rebuild new thoughts in my mind and new beliefs in my heart, but also stop believing the lies of fear I had believed for so long. This took time and discipline, daily reading the Word of God and meditating and thinking upon it until my mind was renewed in truth.

With fear also comes the feelings of dread, thoughts of worry, suspicion, insecurity, distrust, disappointment, all of which are very negative emotions, (this is the short list). There can also be feelings of anger, bad temper, jealousy, often fear will trigger another negative emotion or stir up a reaction in us. I would often react in anger and then realise it was because **fear was behind my reasoning**. This is what I mean by uncovering the root cause.

Our reactions of anger or distrust can be because deep down we feel afraid or there is something else we are concerned about. Often I would get upset with my husband over the smallest things, but behind it was this insecurity and fear I felt. It could have been as simple as him being late from work or staying longer at the church and my mind would begin to work overtime and fear would build up and I would reason something else was going on, when in fact it was all in my head. By the time Graeme, my husband, would get home I would be so upset and angry he didn't know what to do. I was usually too out of control by this stage.

We can be afraid of opening up our hearts for fear of being hurt or misunderstood by others, but to get free we have to confess them and in doing this we are uncovering them and allowing healing to take place. I knew God wanted me well and the way to being well inside and out was to let Him inside my heart and heal my brokenness. I had invited Jesus to live in my heart and to take total control. There is so much more the Lord has for us in our hearts beyond brokenness, pain and suffering, He has come to bring healing.

This Treasure we possess
2 Corinthians 4:7 speaks to us of treasure, this treasure we possess in frail human vessels. This treasure is Jesus. He came to live on the inside of our hearts to transform our hearts and give us the fullness of His life inside and out. We do not have to live out of our own strength and

reasoning, but in the fullness of His grace, love, hope and power. He comes to give us a new heart and a new mind through the out-working of His power in our lives. But we must be willing to cooperate with Him and hand over our old life, old ways of thinking and behaving. It takes obedience and trust to hand our lives over.

Through the trials and tests we encounter we are refined in our character and this builds our faith and dependence in Jesus. Life is full of challenges and crisis can come to anyone of us, it's through this we find out what's really on the inside: faith or fear? Love, hope, perseverance, patience, we are certainly tried in our faith but the Word of God says it is through these trials and the proving of our faith we will lack no good thing (James 1: 1-4, 1 Peter 1:7).

This treasure He speaks of, we find in the Word of God and in our relationship with the Lord Jesus Christ. He daily promises to us, life in abundance to the full and overflowing (John 10:10). We can choose His way of living each day, being dependant on Him and not living out of our own strength and abilities.

I learnt the hard way, by living in my own strength and wearing myself out physically.I had not entrusted every part of my life over to Jesus. This in itself is what faith is all about. Handing our lives over to Him and trusting Him with the greater details. When we decide to entrust our hearts to Him and allow the Holy Spirit to work in us, we can be led and guided by His Word in our lives, thus enabling us to do all things through Christ who strengthens us.

The key is to invite Him in to unlock the hurts of the past or any disappointments or fears of the future and to hand our hearts back to Him to work on us from the inside out. This is our decision, He doesn't force us, it's our choice to invite the Saviour into

> *It takes obedience and trust to hand our lives over.*

our hearts and make us new. By asking Jesus to come live in the centre of our hearts, we are saying, "I want you to be the centre and focus of my life. I want and need a fresh start, to begin a new life." His ability to heal and make us whole is not limited to our past. He washes away the past and makes all things new (2 Cor. 5:17). Then out of this ongoing relationship with Jesus at the centre of our being we begin to live our lives transformed by His amazing grace and power. Remember that He will never leave nor forsake us!

Now there are so many wonderful treasures in the Word of God for you to discover and put into your heart for daily living. They will transform your heart and transform you into a new person. Start by looking over these key Scriptures references about the heart and the inner man:

New Testament—Scripture Keys about the heart

- Ephesians 3: 16, 17—Jesus comes to live in our hearts
- Ephesians 4:22-24—Put on the new man
- Luke 6:45—Out of the heart the mouth speaks
- Matthew 6:21—Where your treasure is your heart is
- Matt 15:18, 19
- John 14:1—Let not your hearts be troubled
- Romans 10:10—With your heart you believe
- 1 Corinthians 2:9
- 1 Peter 3:4
- Proverbs 17:22 & Proverbs 18:14
- Ezekiel 18:31 & 36:36—A new heart

UNCOVER THIS HEART OF MINE

*I've tried so hard to protect this heart of mine, only to see the walls
around me. Held like a captive bird, I only wanted to be free, waiting for
the door to open.*

*Then there was you, who found me, you shone your light around me
revealing your love, inside of my heart.*

*Uncover this heart, of mine, pour in your healing
Uncover this heart of mine,
Uncover this heart of mine bring in your holiness.*

*Now all I see is your light over me and all I know is your love,
You've uncovered, sweet mysteries, Like the morning you awakened me.
No more darkness, no more war, in this heart of mine you're all I'm
living for.*

*I had to let go, get on my knees and pray
You opened my heart took my fears away.*

©Paula Connelly 2005 words and music

Proverbs 4:20-27

"My son, attend to my words; consent and submit to my sayings. Let them not depart from your sight; keep them in the centre of your heart for they are life to those who find them, healing and health to all their flesh. Keep and guard your heart with all vigilance and above all that you guard, for out of it flows the springs of life.

Put away from you false and dishonest speech, and wilful and contrary talk put far away from you. Let your eyes look right on with fixed purpose and let your gaze be straight before you. Consider well the path of your feet, and let all your ways be established and ordered a right. Turn not aside to the right hand or to the left; remove your foot from evil."

"Keep and guard your heart with all vigilance and above all that you guard, for out of it flow the springs of life."
Proverbs 4:23

CHAPTER THREE

ABOVE ALL GUARD
YOUR HEART

~Guard Your Heart~

*T*his Scripture found in Proverbs 4:23 was a major key in receiving my healing. It opened up a new way of living and thinking. It gave me the understanding of how I needed to let go and uncover the wrong things in my heart and replace them with the Truth in the Word of God.

It all starts with us understanding our hearts are the very core and centre of our being. They are what make us who we are. As I have said before, our hearts are like containers, they contain the springs of life or the issues of life. This passage got me thinking about my heart and what was going on inside of me.

Deep inside there can be so much going on and so much hidden. Secrets of the heart amongst our dreams and desires, or as I mentioned despairs and negative emotions we may have in our hearts. When Jesus comes to live in our hearts He takes up residence, He comes to make His home in our hearts (Ephesians 3:16, 17).

The heart is also described as a wellspring, meaning a source of continual supply. The word heart is described as the core, centre or root. It is amazing that the heart is the first organ to develop in a baby in the womb. The source of life begins in the heart. No heartbeat, no life. The heart pumps blood and oxygen to every other organ in our bodies giving them life.

What we speak also reveals our hearts, for out of the abundance of the heart the mouth speaks (Luke 6:45). Therefore, if our hearts are healthy and full of what is good and right then what comes out of us is good, but if our hearts are unhealthy then that's what will flow out. We live out of the thoughts of our hearts reasoning and disputing. What issues are in your heart? In Matthew 15:18-19 it says, *'whatever comes out of the mouth comes from the heart and this is what makes a man unclean and defiles (him).* Therefore what we say reveals our hearts.

What's welling up and flowing out of our hearts?

So what do you have stored up in your heart? The good treasures: love, joy, peace, or unresolved hurts, unbelief and fear? Our hearts can be healed and whole or sick and troubled. It's only when we guard them from the evil and keep the Living Word in our hearts that we truly remain free.

> Luke 6:45 "The upright (honourable, intrinsically good) man out of the good treasure stored in his heart produces what is upright and the evil man or of the evil storehouse brings forth that which is depraved (wicked and intrinsically evil) for out of the abundance (overflow) of the heart his mouth speaks."

We can live a truly prosperous life inside and out by keeping the Word of God in the centre of our hearts. It's what we allow to rule us, whether it is out of our emotions, hurts, fears, or the Holy Spirit and His power that makes all the difference. What we allow into our hearts and minds will be what comes out of us. Good or bad, positive or negative.

What are these issues of life we are to guard from?

What things of life can trouble us? Worry, stress, anxiety, fear, cares of this world. From relationships to finances, raising our families, teenagers, managing our work, careers, ministry and all the things life contains; sickness and crisis times, when things happen that we just don't plan and turn our lives upside down. It can happen to anyone, a crisis or trial, this life has its challenges.

> Matthew 6:25 "Therefore I tell you, stop being perpetually uneasy (anxious and worried) about your life . . ."

But here Jesus tells us to stop being worried and anxious about our everyday lives. He knows what we need and how He will get it to us. The key is to put first the kingdom of God, His way of doing things. By doing this we trust Him to provide all that we need and more.

> Matthew 6:33, 34 *"But seek first of all His kingdom and His righteousness (His way of doing and being right) and then all these things taken together will be given your besides. So do not worry or be anxious about tomorrow, for tomorrow will have worries and anxieties of it own. Sufficient for each day is its own trouble."*

Keeping the Word in the centre of our hearts

What a priceless treasure the Word of God is, more valuable than diamonds and rubies. The Word is God's words of wisdom to us. Nothing in the earth and no one compares to His wisdom. King Solomon asked for wisdom and God gave it to him. Because he had this wisdom from God, he also obtained riches and wealth in his lifetime. The Word of God is God's will for our lives!

When something is so priceless and valuable you keep your eye on it, you won't let it out of your sight. I know I am that way with precious things like jewels and diamonds. They don't come easy so we don't lose sight of them. But the Word is more precious than these. As we endeavour to keep the Word in our sight and not lose sight of the truth it contains, it will continue to bring life and healing to all our flesh.

> Proverbs 4:20-21 *"My Son, attend to my words, consent and submit to my sayings. Let them not depart from your sight; keep them in the centre of your heart."*

The Word of God brings light, illumination, revelation, clear direction, opens the eyes of our understanding, and a sure path to follow. His Word is a lamp unto my feet a light unto my path.

I came to the realization that I had not put the Word of God in the centre of my heart, nor was I completely keeping my eyes on it. I had not allowed Jesus or His Word to be in the centre of my life. I had allowed fear to be the controlling negative force in my heart for so long; it was blocking the way to me living in the fullness of his love, peace and grace. It was in my focus constantly.

I was exhausted from all my own works and striving for perfection. I had not put Jesus in the centre of my concerns and worries. I had always tried to work them out for myself, telling Him what I needed to do. This is an exhausting way to live. **I had allowed the spirit of fear to be a controlling negative force in my life, which made me insecure, suspicious, sensing evil and dread most of the time in my life.** This eventually led to the deterioration of my physical health, panic attacks, severe stress, anger; my emotions were being led out of this fear factor.

> *Proverbs 12:25 "Anxiety in the heart of man weighs him down, but an encouraging word makes it glad . . ."*
>
> *Proverbs 15:13 "A glad heart makes a cheerful countenance, but by sorrow of heart the spirit is broken."*

In all of our life's choices we have a free will to choose to live out of His Love and grace or to do things our own way. For me I had been living out of my own strength and not trusting myself to Jesus daily to handle my cares.

When we hand our fears and anxieties to the Lord and put His Word in their place, our hearts can rest and be assured He has the answers. He is able to meet our needs, He is able to do superabundantly more than we could ever dare dream ask or imagine (Ephesians 3:19, 20).

Just like a little child knows how to trust himself, herself to a loving parent, we need to take the risk and do this with God. It's by faith we do this, releasing those cares in prayer and not even giving them another thought. He is able to do what we cannot do.

How to guard our hearts
The key to guarding our hearts is putting the word into our hearts and

minds. *Proverbs 4:20 says,' My son attend to my words consent and submit to my sayings.' This means to give proper attention to my word.*

When we give attention we are deliberately making note of what it says. We do this by meditating and thinking on the word of God. It's like putting spiritual medicine into our hearts.

There is power in putting the word into our hearts, it not only brings Faith but establishes the truth we need in our hearts that will produce the healing for our hearts, minds and bodies. (3 John 2)

Another key to guarding our hearts is to examine what we truly believe about our lives. What are the convictions we hold within our hearts.

In my situation I had believed for years that I needed to fear something bad , this created feelings of anxiety. It was only when I received the truth about Gods love for me, that I was able to replace the lies that had held me captive for so long. The key here is to stop the lies of the enemy from entering our hearts, by believing what Gods word says about us.

As we meditate and think upon the Word of God, allowing the truth to live in the centre of our hearts, it takes up residence on the inside of us. The Word of God is like medicine to our hearts. Once you take it into your heart the process of healing begins. Guarding our hearts is all about keeping Gods word as the central focus. It's about what we choose to believe as the truth. ***Proverbs 4:21 and 22 says, 'Let them not depart from your sight; keep them in the centre of your heart. For they are life to those who find them, healing and health to all their flesh.'***

By keeping the word in our sights and in our hearts we are able to guard from the lies of the enemy. It's knowing the Truth that makes us free and by this we keep a guard over our hearts.

Practical steps to guarding our hearts
As practical application of getting the word into my heart, I would make time to just sit and read or listen to a cd teaching on faith and healing.

Other times I would just spend time soaking in the presence of God while listening to Praise and worship. I noticed after doing this for a few months the difference on the inside of my heart. I didn't believe the lies of the enemy; I was being transformed and renewed in my heart and mind through the Word of God and what it said. The anxiety began to be less and less, the panic attacks stopped, I was beginning to rest more and the striving ceased. I was living out of the truth and not the lies of the enemy, although at times I still battled in my mind, I was getting stronger in my faith daily by pressing into the Word.

Stop the enemy from entering our minds! Say no to his lies and deceptions.

By putting a guard over our hearts, doesn't mean we put up false walls of protection (to self- protect). It is the opposite, we are to let those false walls of protection down, and allow the Holy Spirit to renew and refresh our hearts. For years I had put up walls in my heart thinking I was self-protecting but I was only hiding fear behind those walls. I thought I could protect myself from being hurt or controlled but instead this fear was controlling me.

In guarding our hearts, we are to stop the enemy from putting his lies into our minds and into our hearts. Don't allow them to enter. This is how we guard. It's no different to stopping a robber from entering into your house. You wouldn't deliberately allow an enemy access. You would lock that front door, and you would call on the authorities to come take that enemy away. It's the same with our hearts; we must call on the authority of the Lord Jesus Christ to come and protect us and shield our hearts from these enemy attacks.

As we call on His Name, all authority has been given to us in heaven and earth to bind up the enemy and to stop him from tampering in our lives and in our hearts. The Word of God is our final authority and what He says about us.

In Mark 16:18 Jesus said, "All authority (all power of rule) in heaven and on earth has been given to Me."

This is how we guard our hearts; we lift up a standard against the enemy, in Jesus Name. Not fighting in our own strength but with the sword of the Spirit, which is this powerful weapon—His Word—speaking it out and believing it with all our hearts.

The Armour of God as our protection and shield

> *Ephesians 6:11-13 "Put on God's whole armour (the armour of a heavy-armed soldier which God supplies), that you may be able successfully to stand up against (all) the strategies and the deceits of the devil. For we are not wrestling with flesh and blood (contending only with physical opponents), but against the despotisms, against the powers, against (the master spirits who are) the world rulers of this present darkness, against the spirit forces of wickedness in the heavenly (supernatural) sphere. Therefore put on God's complete armour, that you may be able to resist and stand your ground on the evil day (of danger) and having done all (the crisis demands) to stand, (firmly in your place)."*

The rest of Ephesians 6:14-17 explains the pieces of armour God has supplied for us: The belt of truth, breastplate of righteousness, the feet of peace, shield of faith, helmet of salvation and the sword of the Spirit which is the Word of God. When we are dressed and ready in this spiritual armour of God we are prepared when the enemy's attacks come to our hearts and minds. We are ready to extinguish every evil flaming arrow from the enemy and turn those evil thoughts away.

Guarding our minds
In the same way we guard our hearts by putting in the Word, we guard our minds by putting renewed thoughts into our minds. We need to think about what we are thinking about!

> *Romans 12:2 "Do not be conformed to this world (this age) fashioned after and adapted to its external, superficial customs), but be transformed (changed) by the entire renewal of your mind (by its new ideals and it new attitude), so that you may prove (for yourselves) what is the good and acceptable and perfect will of God, even the thing which is good and acceptable and perfect (in His sight for you)."*

Therefore we are not to conform, or pattern our lives after the world's ways of living but after God's way. This means being renewed in our minds daily through; reading the Word, study and meditation on the scriptures. Even a passage a day will bring light and illumination to our hearts. (Ephesians 4:23)

The most important thing to remember is that we have been given the Holy Spirit as our helper and comforter in this life to teach us, guide us and lead us into all Truth.

Guard what we say!

I used to be a very negative person, always saying something negative or having a slant of negativity on things. The Bible says life and death are in the power of the tongue.

> *Proverbs 18:21 "Death and life are in the power of the tongue, and they who indulge in it shall eat the fruit of it (for death or life)."*

> *We can speak life or death over ourselves—choose life this day!*

Guarding what we say is vital to a healthy inside out life. We have the power to speak the promises of God over our lives or we can speak negatively and death. My Mum would say to us when we were young, 'if you can't say anything nice then don't say anything at all.' Good advice! We must bridle our tongues and train them to talk right about ourselves and our situations, and about others. It can be so easy to agree with your feelings. Oh I don't feel well today, or I feel so tired, complaining can come easy to us. God's words are powerful and they are life to all our flesh, but just the same negative words have power and they bring death—death to our hearts and minds.

This is not just about speaking positive but speaking the truth over our lives and what the Word of God says. For years the devil had spoken into my ears words of fear and dread, thoughts would come into my mind and terrify me. I had to replace those thoughts and words with Truth and what God said about me.

Words of life and healing are what I began to speak over my heart. Ever noticed when you are around positive optimistic people that you just feel better having spent time with them, but negative people can drag you down. I make a point now to get around Godly optimistic people who are full of life, those that are not so optimistic we can certainly encourage them by being the life giver. It's the same within our own hearts; we can speak life into our own hearts and situations or death to them.

I remember clearly one day getting out of bed when I was really struggling with the fatigue, I was in the habit of saying "I'm so tired" but I felt the Lord speak to my heart and tell me to say, "The Lord is my strength, I can do all things through Christ who strengthens me." As I began to say this out loud, I realised within about ten minutes I was actually feeling strength in my body. I made a conscious effort every morning to stop myself saying how tired I was and replacing it with: I have strength in Jesus' Name. It's not a magic potion, but the truth is—what we say is what we believe and receive.

I would rather speak the Word of God than negativity any day. I had discovered speaking a whole new way over my body and I was seeing a transformation. I had to do this by faith and as I did my body soon became stronger and back to normal again.

The other thing I suggest is writing up these Scriptures and hanging them around your house, on your fridge or mirrors in your bathroom, read them out and meditate upon them; they will get deep into your heart until it's the only thing you believe.

> *Psalm 27 "The Lord is my Light and my salvation, whom shall I fear or dread? The Lord is the refuge and stronghold of my life—of whom shall I be afraid."*

When the Word is in our mouth and we speak out God's truth and promises, then what we speak becomes reality in our lives. This is not a magic spell, but as we strongly make a decision to speak directly over our lives Gods word, it will change how we think and what we believe. I like what David the Psalmist says in Psalm 34, 'I will bless the Lord at all times; His praise shall continually be in my mouth.' This is a decision of his will to praise and bless and not to complain or speak evil.

Here is a list of Psalms to speak out over your life, for daily blessings and meditation:

- Psalm 19:14: "Let the words of my mouth and the meditation of my heart, be acceptable in your sight; O Lord my Rock and my Redeemer."
- *Proverbs 13:3 "He who guards his mouth keeps his life, but he who opens wide his lips comes to ruin."*
- *Proverbs 16: 24 "Pleasant words are as a honeycomb, sweet to the mind and healing to the body."*
- *Proverbs 15:4 "A gentle tongue (with its healing power) is a tree of life, but wilful contrariness in it breaks down the spirit."*
- Psalm 27
- Psalm 40
- Psalm 37
- Psalm 16

Guarding what we see

Getting distracted is so easy, staying focused takes discipline. Like an athlete focusing on the finish line, we must look straight ahead to the things that God has for us.

> *Hebrews 12:1-3 "Therefore then since we are surrounded by so great a cloud of witnesses let us strip off and throw aside every encumbrance (unnecessary weight) and that sin which so readily (deftly and cleverly) clings to and entangles us, and let us run with patient endurance and steady and active persistence the appointed course of the race that is set before us. Looking away from all that will distract to Jesus, who is the leader and the source of our faith and is also its finisher . . ."*

This simply means don't look to the left or to the right but straight ahead towards the goal that is in Jesus our Saviour (Philippians 3:14). Not looking to the past And all that was wrong but focusing on the present and to the future we have in Christ. Keeping our eyes fixed on Him and all He has done. By putting our trust in Him in our hearts, minds, what we say, see, think, feel, we are taking responsibility for our hearts and what we allow into them, only putting that which is good and truth into our hearts is the key.

Guarding from the negative emotions, worries and stresses of life

Instead of having our worries as the focus and in the centre of our hearts, we focus on the Word of God. Imagine with me for a moment a large mountain. See it? It's huge depending on how close you are to that mountain—it may look bigger or smaller. When we put our problems in our view it's like this. If they are the main focus, what we think upon all day long, they become so close they obstruct our view staring us right in the face, we can't see anything but the problem, because it looks so huge to overcome. But if we move back a bit, stop thinking on it all of the time by casting our cares over to God—the problem shrinks and gets smaller in our sight. We have to see this problem through God's eye view, which is His Word.

If we are worrying all the time this simply means the problem is on our minds. We can get into reasoning and trying to work it out all by ourselves, and just end up more worried. Or we could simply trust God and release our cares to Him.

What we need to do is speak to our Mountains!

We can speak about the mountain or to the mountain.

> **Mark 11: 23** *"Truly I tell you, whoever says to this mountain, be lifted up and thrown into the sea! And does not doubt at all in his heart but believes that what he says will take place, it will be done for him."*

What an amazing verse for us to take into our hearts and believe. Speak to your mountain (your problem) and tell it to go in Jesus Name. The key is to believe that God is able to do this in our lives, realising we are empowered through the Word of God to speak to those mountains and obstacles, overcoming them in His strength and grace. The key is speaking the word of God and not the problem.

Get the problem out of your focus and off your mind by speaking the word instead. Your victory is in Jesus' Name. Even if you don't see it at first instance in the natural, see your victory by faith. This is how we are to pray and believe for Gods promises to come into being.

> **Hebrews 11 :1** *"Now faith is the assurance (the confirmation, the title deed) of the things we hope for, being the proof of things we do not see and the conviction of their reality (faith perceiving as real fact what is not revealed to our senses)."*

It is by faith we obtain the promises of God. Without faith it is impossible to please God.

> **Hebrews11:6** *But without faith it is impossible to please and be satisfactory to Him. For whoever would come near to God must (necessarily) believe that God exists and that He is the rewarder of those who earnestly and diligently seek Him (out).*

We can guard what we see by watching what we watch on television or read in the news or on the Internet. There are so many avenues to watching negative evil reports but it's up to us to put into our minds and heart God's Word and the things that will benefit our lives. It's like with our diet and eating habits; junk in, junk out, it just makes you sick. However when we put good healthy food into our diets, the benefits are much better for your physical body and whole life. There is a saying, *'What you eat, you become.'*

What you read, think, speak and believe you also become. For us to live a truly new life in Christ we must be putting the Word of God into our hearts daily and meditating and thinking upon it.

> *3 John 2 "Beloved, I pray that you may prosper in every way and that your body may keep well, even as I know you soul keeps well and prospers."*

As I conclude this chapter, I would like to suggest an important step in obtaining freedom (within our hearts). That is to go to a trusted pastor, leader, or Christian counsellor that will pray with you and believe with you for resolve in these issues. (James 5:16)

There is power through confession to one another and prayer, upon which we can receive the love and forgiveness of God. If we allow any unforgiveness, or bitterness to stay in our hearts (or take root in our hearts), it can be the very thing blocking the way for our complete healing. Jesus urges us to cast the whole of our cares upon Him.

Finally, to continue living with hearts that are free from fears and the negatives of life or from being ruled by any negative emotions, we must abide in the Word of God, putting our complete trust and confidence in Him. This is not a works thing; it's a matter of trusting our hearts to Jesus daily in prayer. He is able then to keep our hearts and guard them and renew us daily in His Word bringing transformation to our lives.

For all sickness and disease, whether emotional, mental or physical, Jesus is our healer today. As you begin to study the Scriptures starting with the Gospels, you will see that Jesus went about healing all who were sick and oppressed. **Jesus has come to heal the broken hearted and set the captives free!**

Isaiah 61:1-2

The Spirit of the Lord God is upon me, because the Lord has anointed and qualified me to preach the Gospel of good tidings to the meek the poor, and afflicted; He has sent me to bind up and heal the broken hearted, to proclaim liberty to the (physical and spiritual) captives and the opening of the prison and of the eyes to those who are bound. To proclaim the acceptable year of the Lord (the year of His favour) and the day of vengeance of our God to comfort all who mourn.

"True courage is the ability to face obstacles in life and do them even if you are afraid."

CHAPTER FOUR

NO FEAR!

~What Would You Do If You Had No Fear?~

I can see it now; the hopes, the dreams, the adventures, and the risks we would take. That business you desired to start, the mountains to climb, the oceans to sail, the songs to write, the world to discover. A life flourishing with no fear, marriages hot and passionate, relationships with no fear—imagine that! Maybe you have desired to do something but fear has held you back. I am here to cheer you on and say run, go do that thing that is in your heart and don't let fear stop you! **Get out of the box that has contained you and take that step of faith.** Jump out of the boat and walk on the water as Peter did (Matthew 14: 24-32).

> *God has not given to us a spirit of fear!*

As I have said, for many years fear was a controlling force in my life until I received the revelation that fear is not from God, for He has not given to us a spirit of fear! 2Timothy1:7 Sometimes we have to delve into the deepest darkest parts of our hearts to face our fears, and in this we find out who we really are. It's then we discover that these fears are a mere shadow trying to intimidate us and a shadow can do us no harm.

> *He created all things for us and us for greater things.*

In order to overcome my fears I had to be willing to step out of my comfort zones and everything that was familiar to me, into the realm of the unknown.

In doing this I found out there was so much more waiting for me. It's the mystery of the soul, we fear what we do not know and we can be afraid of embarking on the journey of our dreams because of the uncertainty we feel but if we stay safe because of fear we will never find out what God really has for us. We must dare to take those steps of faith regardless of the fear we feel. As we step into this unknown territory, even if mountains of fear are trying to stare us down we will come into our very destiny and purpose in life. Did you know once you obtain truth and knowledge about a matter fear is no longer the problem? Sometimes it's just the fear of the unknown that scares us. Get knowledge and get wisdom instead of fear.

This is what it means to have courage: to be able to live your life to the fullest degree whether or not you feel afraid and to decide (regardless of the fears) that you are going to do all that is in your heart.

> *For God hath not given us the spirit of fear, but of power and of love and of a sound mind. 2 Timothy1:7 (NKJV)*

Greater is our God

Our God is great and mighty and through Him we can do all things. He created all things for us and us for greater things. He loves us more than we will ever understand or comprehend. God is our Father in heaven who longs for us to take the precious promises of His Word and put them into action in our lives. He created man in His image to do great works on the earth and that means without fear (John 14:12, 13). We just have to be willing to take those steps of faith and even if we doubt or begin to sink (like Peter), know that Jesus will pull us right up again. It's in trusting Him that we eliminate fear from our lives.

Fear was my guide for many years

I know what it's like to go to bed trembling with fear and waking with thoughts of fear as my guide, ever tormenting and pulling me under its power. For over twenty-five years I lived with this perspective of fear. I thought it was normal to feel fear as I did, therefore from childhood into adulthood I accepted this way of thinking. It was as though I had this sense of dread and evil, or danger crouching at my door almost all of the time. It was a feeling that something bad was about to happen. I realized that in my mind I had constant thoughts of dread, never feeling safe, waiting for the worst to happen. I was certainly not very optimistic about life. I would ask my husband if he felt this way and had these kinds of thoughts of fear, he said he rarely did. So what was it with me?

Unfortunately, this is where through the fear and anxiety, my physical body couldn't take anymore and under the stress and constant worry, my mind, emotions and body finally gave way. The shaking and the panic attacks started regularly occurring, accompanied by dizziness and fatigue. My body was completely burnt out. Fear was underneath the surface deep in my heart waiting to bring its destructive powers. I knew it was there but I didn't know how to stop thinking the way I did or control the fear I felt. It had become such a pattern of thinking that it was almost what made me feel safe. I felt better about thinking the worst than I did expecting something good, just in case the worst happened I was alert and ready. On guard for all the wrong reasons, I was in a state of constant self-protection. What a major deception this was in my mind.

I'm thankful that Jesus Christ came to my rescue in this dark hour. I was not alone after all, He was there waiting to hold me in the night hours, to calm my fears and still my heart from dread and terror.

> *Psalm 34:4 "I sought (inquired of) the Lord and required Him (of necessity and on the authority of His Word) and he heard me and delivered me from all my fears."*

God heard my cry for help and set me free from this evil tormenting spirit of fear. Through these pages I will explain how I was set free from being controlled by fear.

Perfect love casts out all fear!
The perfect love of Jesus Christ is the answer to all our fears. There is no fear in His perfect love; fear does not exist in His love, it cannot exist! (1 John 4:18). WOW, what a wonderful truth. God revealed this to me, and it is my hope many others will come to discover this same truth in their hearts. God's greatest desire is for us to come to know His great love, how high, how deep, how wide and everlasting it is (Romans 8: 35-39). God is Love and fear does not have any place in His love for us.

I had to be willing to trust God with my whole heart and that meant trust in His love and protection plan. The hardest part can be in the area of trust, if you have been hurt before or been in an abusive relationship, trusting God the father will take some time but as you keep your heart open He will reveal the truth you need.

The evil ruler of this world

On the opposite side of things is the devil, he is the ruler of fear and there is no love in him. The enemy (Satan) attempts to bring fear and intimidation into our lives to cause us to shrink back and stop us from living a life full and complete in the love of Jesus Christ. Fear affects our relationships, our walk of faith, and our desire to fulfil our dreams and can affect our outlook on life.

I realized I was not a very optimistic person, I always thought the worst was going to happen. I tried to be positive, but deep down I would question whether I deserved to be blessed. I know now this was because fear brings with it a sense of punishment (1 John 4:18).

For so many years the enemy had me thinking I had something to fear. Fear for my family, fear for my future, and fear of ill health or death. We can have the fear of failure, fear of not

> *As you keep your heart open He will reveal the truth you need.*

doing what we are called to do, fear of being hurt or being let down and therefore not have the courage to step out and do what's in our hearts.

This is how the devil operates in people's lives, by putting his evil thoughts of dread, fear and danger into their hearts and minds. It is a master-ruling spirit and if allowed into our hearts and minds, we can come under its power. Once there, it can stop us from operating out of faith, hope and love.

Today, millions upon millions of people live in fear. Fear is in the atmosphere of the world we live in. Television, and in particular, news items, can be a carrier of fear into our lives. These reports can filter into our minds and belief systems and we can easily believe we are meant to fear certain things. Fear can also come into our hearts and minds through our own life's experiences, crisis times, or we can be taught to fear. Without knowing it, parents can teach their children to fear.

In reality in our society with all of its imperfections, dysfunctional family life, and evil, fear is ever present and active in our earthly realm. The prince of this world, the devil, aims to bring people under his intimidating power and spirit of fear. It comes into our minds as anxiety, worry, insecurity, dread, sense of evil forebodings or sense of danger and brings along with it doubt, wavering, reasoning, confusion and instability. Fear makes us unsure and uncertain about things and leaves us feeling unsafe. To feel fear is one thing but to live in fear is another?

We can all feel afraid or fearful at any given time in our life, but we are not to be controlled by it as a stronghold in our hearts and minds. For example, hearing a loud noise may frighten a child; this is entirely different to living under a spirit of fear. God was revealing this to me through this time in my life.

Another aspect of fear is to intimidate. This means to make timid or fearful, to compel or deter as if by threats. Other words used to describe intimidation are to bully, bulldoze, to cower implies; reduction to a state where the spirit is broken or all courage is lost. To bulldoze is to urge, make demands and threats through aggressive behaviour, which is bullying. This is how the enemy comes to bully and threaten us with his lies and deceptions to make us cowardly and afraid.

We can feel fear and stop it from being a controlling force, tell it to leave and turn to God for peace in those times. When we do not take authority over the fear it becomes anxiety and worry in our hearts and minds, stealing the peace that God has for us. **We have authority in Jesus' Name to cast out all fear** and we do this by living out of the Truth in His word and standing on the authority of the Word of God.

The fear of 'What if'
I would like to say I overcame fear overnight, but the truth is I had a stronghold in my mind that needed to be broken and renewed. Wrong thought patterns and beliefs had been ingrained in my mind and heart for so long it took some time for me to get a new perspective and understanding about my life. I had to spend much of my time renewing my mind and changing my thinking patterns in respect to fear.

This stronghold of fear in my mind affected the way I responded in certain situations, what I believed about myself and my future and mostly the thoughts I was thinking daily. The Bible says to take captive every thought that is not from God. That means every lying thought, and every argument and reasoning thought. To take it captive is to stop thinking it and to replace it with the Word of truth.

> *2 Corinthians 10:4, 5 "For the weapons of our warfare are not physical (weapons of flesh and blood), but they are mighty before God for the overthrow and destruction of strongholds. (Inasmuch as we) refute arguments and theories and reasoning's and every proud lofty thing that sets itself up against the true knowledge of God; and we lead every thought and purpose away captive into the obedience of Christ (the Messiah the anointed one)."*

I had a habitual thought pattern of, 'What if this or that happens or doesn't happen?' 'What if I get a terminal illness or my husband gets ill or someone gets hurt, how will we cope?' Or other scenarios like, 'What if we don't have enough money to pay the bills, what if we go on this holiday and it rains for the whole two weeks or one of the kids get sick or something bad happens to us?' You can see how these thoughts only bring worry and torment. These kinds of thoughts steal your peace and joy and your ability to live in today, always worrying about tomorrow.

They also bring uncertainty about our future or the present and can make us anxious and upset all the time, which was how I was on the inside.

> *Proverbs 12:25 "Anxiety in a man's heart weighs him down, but an encouraging word makes it glad."*

I was always anxious about tomorrow, when tomorrow hadn't even arrived. I was the kind of person who was worrying and striving for tomorrow but not knowing how to live in peace today. The Bible tells us that the birds of the air don't worry and God provides for them. Why worry then? Matthew 6:25-34 tells us, *'Be anxious for nothing!'*

> **We have authority in Jesus' Name to cast out all fear.**

As I have already mentioned, we are to pull down every thought and imagination, every argument and theory that comes into our mind from the enemy. That includes anxious thoughts. Have you ever noticed a time when you had conflicting dreadful thoughts going on in your head; whilst the voice of the Holy Spirit is quietly saying, 'Stay in peace or don't worry.' We need to discern the thoughts of fear that come from the enemy (to oppress us), then by pulling them down and throwing them off we can hear the Holy Spirit's voice clearly. As we keep our thoughts on the word of God our minds are kept in perfect peace. *Isaiah 26:3*

Another verse in Ephesians 4:23-24 says to be constantly renewed in the spirit of your mind (having a fresh mental and spiritual attitude), and put on the new nature (regenerate self) created in God's image in true righteousness and holiness.

Put on the new mind in Christ
We are instructed to put off the old nature and put on the new mind of Christ, which we receive when we read the Word of God. In this we are being changed and renewed in the way we think about ourselves, the situations we face, and it gives us God's perspective and wisdom for our lives. It's as simple as us making the decision to put out of our minds the old way of thinking and like putting on clothes daily, we put on our new spiritual attitude and wear this on our hearts and minds. It's the new life Jesus came and modelled for us.

As we keep our minds set and focused on what's above (Colossians 3:2), thinking on the Word of God and the truth that He brings; our minds and hearts will be lifted up and renewed, flowing with peace. But if we keep thinking on our problems our minds stay low and we become depressed and fearful and there is no peace in our minds. It's a choice to think about what you are thinking about. We choose our thoughts.

> **Philippians 4:8** *"Finally brethren, whatever things are true, whatever things are noble, whatever things are just whatever things are pure whatever things are lovely whatever things are of good report if there is any virtue and if there is anything praiseworthy—meditate on these things."*

Fear versus wisdom

Fear can seem to be a sensible reaction to certain situations. For example, we recently took a trip overseas and that country was experiencing civil unrest at the time. Due to the news reports my parents were alarmed and expressed some fear about us going. This is where we need the wisdom of God and His discernment in our hearts to guide us. We can choose wisdom over fear.

> **Psalm 23:4** *"Yes though I walk through the valley of the shadow of death I will fear or dread no evil for You are with me; Your rod (to protect) and Your staff (to guide) they comfort me."*

We did not feel fearful about going and as we prayed and asked for the Lord's protection, we had peace in our hearts to continue with our plans. It turned out there was plenty of protection where we were staying and we did not encounter any danger. In fact we sat next to the head of security for the united nation in that region on our flight over and he assured us of the safety that was being provided. We were able to report this back to our family and everyone was glad to hear our good news.

It may seem normal to fear this kind of thing, but this is where we can ask God for wisdom and peace in these situations and this expels all fear. Proverbs 4:6 says, *'forsake not wisdom and she will keep, defend and protect you; love her and she will guard you.'*

Wisdom will guard and protect us we have no need of fear.

We choose whether or not we will operate in fear or wisdom. All of us at some point in our lives will experience fear, but we can stop it from becoming a stronghold in our lives by casting our cares upon the Lord and by trusting in the Word of God and His love for us.

I have become aware in my own family to constantly build love and faith and to establish no unhealthy fear in our children's lives. Even though I have made plenty of mistakes in the early stages, it is never too late to start rebuilding new patterns of thinking and believing now for each and every one of us. We have a new saying in our family: **No fear lives here!** Every single day we can choose to stop fear from being entertained in our minds, homes, or from being a controlling force in our lives. Let's choose NO FEAR!

How does Jesus calm our fears?

Jesus and his disciples decide to go across the sea in a boat, but a violent storm begins to toss the boat about, so that the waves are crashing against it. As you could

God will lead us upon the right path.

imagine, this is a frightening scene. But the amazing thing is that the disciples find Jesus asleep in the boat. Upon awakening Him and calling to him to save them, He says to them; "Why are you timid and afraid, O you of little faith?" Then He got up and rebuked the winds and the sea, and there was a great and wonderful calm (Matthew 8:23-26).

Immediately Jesus responds with authority over the storm and stills the wind and the sea and brings peace to the whole situation. I believe this is a picture for us to not allow the storms in our lives to rule our hearts with fear and to speak peace to them and for each one of us to live calm, well—balanced lives from the inside out. This stops us from becoming fearful, fretting or anxious by taking authority over these situations, just as Jesus did in this storm. Jesus has given us this same authority in our lives.

It has never been God's intention for us to live in fear. He knows that fears stop us from living a life of faith and from fully trusting in His love for us. As I have said the enemy, Satan, is the giver of all fear, dread, and terror in this world. He is the evil ruler of this world, he aims to intimidate people and stop us from living a life of faith, hope and love.

Fear and insecurity

With fear comes insecurity. This can make us doubt and live a rollercoaster type of life, unstable and unsure of our surrounds. Being insecure makes it hard to make clear decisions because fear is always ruling the outcome of those decisions. At times I would be wanting to make a decision and so many opposing thoughts would come in to my mind, it wouldn't matter what I wanted to do I felt afraid that something would go wrong.

I had to stop being like this and trust God with my decisions right or wrong that He would guide me and He would look after us in the outcomes. Now when I make decisions I have learnt that God's peace accompanies me and as I follow His peace, my heart and mind stay in peace. If anything becomes unsure, I know to stop and wait for God's peace before I go ahead. Sitting on the fence brings indecision, so once we make a decision God will lead us upon the right path. His Word is a lamp unto my feet and a light unto my path (Psalm 119:105). We can put our trust in God to direct us and lead us at all times. He is faithful and will not fail us.

Fear or faith?

> "Do not fear for I am with you."

Faith is the assurance (the confirmation, the title deed) of things we hope for, being the proof of thing we do not see and conviction of their reality (Hebrews 11:1). With faith comes confidence, trust, reliance, courage, assurance of things hoped for and so much more in Christ whom we can depend on. When our faith is firmly established in him and founded in Him securely we are certain and sure He will do what we cannot do. God is faithful to His promises; He is able to bring them to pass. We are called to live a life of faith and confidence in our God and do great exploits for Him. We must believe with God all things are possible (Luke 1:37).

Faith=courage

The definition of courage means to have mental or moral strength to venture, persevere, and withstand danger, fear or difficulty. Courage implies firmness of mind and will in the face of danger and extreme difficulty (Webster's Dictionary meaning).

It's like saying I will set my mind firmly on the Lord, I take courage because I know that God is with me. As we place our trust firmly in Him, fear cannot take hold of our hearts and minds.

As I have read and studied the scriptures and references to fear, I have discovered that every time God would appear through an angel to give instruction to someone He would announce to them, *'Do not fear, for I am with you.'* The first thing God spoke to them about was not having fear, or not being afraid. He always gave them this sure direction that He was with them and there was nothing to fear. God knows us and our inadequacies, therefore He provides us with all the emotional, spiritual, physical and mental ability and strength that we need for the task. So many times throughout my journey of recovery I would wonder how am I going to get through all of this, but now I am out the other side and I can see how God came to my rescue and strengthened me through the most difficult time of my life.

When the angel visited Mary to tell her she was chosen to be the mother of the Saviour of the world, these are the words he used: *Luke 1:28-30 "Do not be afraid, Mary for you have found grace with God."*

Often when we are faced with a difficult situation or task our first thought is to fear or feel inadequate for the job, but here God is saying to Mary He will do it through her, and this is the same for us. It takes fearless courage to walk and live a life of faith. This is why the enemy comes to oppose our faith with fear, for it is his desire that we do not fulfil God's promises in our lives.

1 John 4:19, we love Him because He first loved us. There is nothing God wouldn't do for us; He loves us beyond our own understanding. If we spent more time studying the love of God and receiving the love of God we would surely abolish all fear from our lives. Perfect love casts out all fear!

It's all about Love
Most importantly the key is for us to replace the lies of fear with the truth of God's love for us. Through confession and prayer we release these lies

and then again by accepting what God's word says about Love, we accept the truth to take place in our hearts.

> *Ephesians 3:17 "May Christ through your faith (actually) dwell (settle down, abide, make His permanent home) in your hearts! May you be rooted deep in love and founded securely on love."*

I was on a journey of discovering the love of God, and in order for me to know it, in my heart; I had to deal with the deep-rooted fear that was blocking that complete understanding of His true love for me. Love empowers us but fear causes us to shrink back.

The way to become deeply rooted in the love of Jesus Christ is to continually receive it through what the Word of God says about His love for us. We need to think and meditate upon His love for us and take it into our hearts through believing. Jesus came to the earth to reveal His true love for us and His plan of Love for every single person on the planet.

We all need to be loved and to love in return, this is what is on the inside of every person and the enemy satan has distorted love and perverted this truth in the earth, causing destruction in many people's lives. Jesus has one command and that is to love one another as He loved us. Imagine if we actually did this for each other? The world would be a different place. Fear would be abolished forever. Not only did Jesus come to bring His love into our hearts but He also came to give us the greatest life we could ever hope for.

Love is the greatest of all gifts. Even faith without love is useless because love is the strength behind our faith and the foundation upon which Jesus commissioned us to build our lives upon. Without faith we cannot please God, because faith requires us to put our hope confidence and trust in God's love for us. So faith and love work together, and together they are powerful against the enemy. **Faith as small as a mustard seed is all that is required to move mountains in our life**.

Faith and fear don't mix. On so many occasions I have pulled myself up when I have been praying for a certain thing and realised I was in fear and worry doubting that He would do it. It's important that when we pray, we believe that God will answer, for what we say and believe in faith God will accomplish (Mark 11:22-24). Fear opposes our faith. Fear can also bring a sense of punishment, and you can have an underlying belief that you deserve something bad to happen. When we think like this we are not grounded in God's love for us. Once you pray just give thanks to God for that thing, we don't have to worry on it anymore.

Family Curse

Satan had been filling my life with fear from a very young age. Growing up I had learned to fear, though I have a wonderful family now, my family had a lot of strife and trouble when I was young. For my parents, marriage was a battleground. This is what I came to expect in my own future and marriage. It had become a way of thinking, a battle in my heart and mind. I feared losing my husband and later as children came along, I feared I would lose them too.

I have four sisters and one brother, and we all grew up very close to each other. I am the youngest of the girls and my brother the youngest in the family. When we were young we all slept in the one room. Our family worked hard, my parents had owned and operated several businesses at different times but we still struggled financially. Times were tough for them.

Often when there was fighting going on, us four kids would get into bed together and my eldest sister would try to calm us down and tell us everything would be ok. You just never knew how things were going to turn out for our family, whether we would have enough money, or food, or whether my parents would stay together. We worried about everything. I can remember if things were not good at home, we would all do what we could to make things better, we would clean the house for our parents and try to keep everything in order so nothing would upset them. As a result, I grew up as a bit of a control freak. If I could control everything and everyone I somehow felt safe. But this brought a lot of trouble with it as growing up and in when I started my own family. I began to relive the same strife and pain my family suffered.

As an adult I became very controlling over my own family (out of this fear factor in my life), if I could control everything I felt safe. I am not blaming my parents for what happened to me, as an adult I realise that we all have difficult times in our finances, raising a family and in our marriages. Naturally, life will have its challenges. The bottom line is that we must take responsibility for our own actions, and although we encounter these difficulties we can open the door of fear or we can open our hearts to trusting God with the whole of our life and all of our cares.

Through fear we can also hinder and bind up our relationships with people if we are operating out of insecurity or manipulating people to get what we want. For many years I was not operating out of God's love and protection, I was desperately trying to control everyone so I felt safe, I didn't realise I was manipulating them in the process because I felt so insecure in who I was. Because I felt this way, most of the time being led by my insecurity, I was a very controlling aggressive person. This was my way of protecting them and keeping us all together. I worked hard on this, as it was a fulltime job constantly keeping everyone under wraps. Even if we went on holidays I couldn't relax, I was on alert for the danger that may happen. I know this sounds crazy but it became an incredible stronghold in my mind. I didn't know how to think positively, I thought if I thought different I wasn't living in reality. As God began to show me the depth of the fears and how it was controlling my life so dangerously and how I was controlling my family, I became aware I did not really trust in His love or plan for me or my family.

This life of fear, made me suspicious, jealous and angry, especially if my husband didn't comply with my demands. It was clear I was not rooted or grounded in the love of Jesus Christ. Not only is this kind of life exhausting to keep up with, it was mentally and emotionally draining on myself and everyone else. This fear also caused strife in our early years of marriage because of the way I would react to situations. The fear drove me in every area of my life; I was always striving to keep everything in order. I was insecure with most relationships and because of this I didn't really trust anyone. I always had my guard in, just in case I was going to get hurt or disappointed. I had my husband and family wrapped up in a nice package just the way I wanted them all to be, the only problem was no one was free to be who they wanted to be.

To top it all off, because of my aggressive Type A personality I would often react to fear with angry outbursts. It's a good thing to ask ourselves why we are angry. As I have said in the earlier chapters we have to get to the root, the real source of the problem to find our healing. Anger may be the reaction or the emotion, but generally fear is the root.

Fear as you can see will cause all kinds of problems, I am only able to speak about this freely because I have been set free from this stronghold and come to recognise how it functions and how debilitating it was in my life. My personal mission is to tell people that God wants them free from being controlled by a spirit of fear and its torment, so each of us can do all that is within our hearts for the Lord without any fear. Thankfully, my parents were saved, restored and have been married for 54 years. God has completely restored my whole family; He has made all things new!

Can we live free from fear?

Jesus has come to set us free from the enemy and from the curse of sin and death. The answer is yes we can live free from the controlling powers of fear. From the beginning God made us to live in dominion. God gave Adam and Eve absolute dominion and authority over everything he had created (Genesis 1:28).

In Matthew 10:1, Jesus summons his disciples and gives them power and authority over unclean spirits, to cure all kinds of diseases and all kinds of weakness and infirmity. We will only live in this authority as we live rooted and grounded in His love for us (Ephesians 3:16-18).

As Jesus Christ Himself makes His home in our hearts and fills us with His love, we are secure in all that He is. We too have dominion over the enemy through the love of Jesus. Jesus has come to set all free from the oppression of the enemy.

Each of us can do all that is within our hearts for the Lord without any fear.

Sometimes because of our past experiences we may find it hard to put our trust in God, we compare Him to the people who have hurt us. But the love of the Saviour does not compare to any human love in the earth. He has come, not to judge

63

but to save, to heal and restore all those who have been lost, hurt and broken. He comes to heal the broken hearted and set the captives free (Isaiah 61).

I found it hard at first to comprehend and understand how much He loved me, but as I persisted in reading the Word and asking for understanding, one day the fullness of this revelation just hit my heart. **The Holy Spirit opened my eyes to the truth and He will do the same for you.** Even if you don't feel anything, God is faithful to meet our needs. He heard my cry for help and now I am healed. The same can happen in your life. In receiving His love, you may need to release forgiveness toward those who have hurt you or disappointed you, this way you leave no foothold for the enemy or blockages in the heart. God wants to turn out all matters of fear from our lives through His abiding love. As we release those who have wronged us, God will take over our hearts with His abiding love and wash away all our hurts and fears. You can learn to live in His love and promises daily by renewing your mind in the living word of God and His truth.

Take a risk with God's love!
Love takes risks, faith takes risks, I don't know how long it has been since you have taken a risk with God, but may I suggest taking a risk and allowing Jesus' love into your heart. When we abide in His amazing love forgiveness flows, grace flows; healing takes place as we keep yielding our hearts to Him. Love takes risks even when our trust has been broken through a person or situation. In order to be free we must be willing to love and trust again.

I can't count how many times I have been betrayed, or left out, or misunderstood by people, but I know that as I keep giving all my cares to the Lord He helps me to build trusting loving relationships again with no fear involved. **Fear wants to protect itself and put up false walls but this only encloses our hearts from the truth and keeps us in darkness.** I had to learn to trust again, in my marriage and with my children. In fact God puts people in your life just to show you just how much you really trust him. Sometimes they can be difficult people and difficult situations but they test our trust in God. You may not be able to trust certain people, but can we trust God even within those circumstances? Yes we can. He will protect us, He will provide the answer we need or how to deal with the person or the situation. It's allowing God to take care of you.

This was the case for me in ministry. I had to hand everything over to others and trust them to do my job, and allow them to be in charge and make the decisions while I was away. I wasn't in control, but this was a great lesson of trust for me to learn. I have become a lot more trusting and forgiving over this time because I have learnt that I can't control everything, everything is in God's hands, not mine. Even with the leadership placed over my life I had to learn to trust that they had my best interests at heart.

The Bible clearly says that God puts leaders over us to watch over us, even if at times they challenge us and we don't like their advice. The truth is any relationship has

> *Love takes risks, faith takes risks.*

to be founded on love and trust. We must ensure that we don't distrust people because of our past experiences; **we must learn to take a risk and trust that God will guide us** in our relationships with others.

Remember that although man is not perfect, GOD is and we can trust him with our lives.

> *David the Psalmist describes it this way in Psalm 118:6-7: "The Lord is on my side; I will not fear what man can do to me? The Lord is on my side and takes my part, He is among those who help me; therefore I shall see my desire established upon those who hate me. It is better to trust and take refuge in the Lord than to put my confidence in man." (Amplified Bible)*

> *Romans 8: 35 "Who shall ever separate us from Christ's love?*
> *Shall suffering and affliction and tribulation? Or calamity and*
> *distress? Or persecution or hunger or destitution or peril or*
> *sword? Yet amid all these things we are more than conquerors*
> *and gain a surpassing victory through Him who loved us. For I*
> *am persuaded beyond doubt (am sure) that neither death nor*
> *life, nor angels nor principalities, nor things impending and*
> *threatening nor things to come nor power nor height nor depth,*
> *nor anything in all creation will be able to separate us from the*
> *love of God which is in Christ Jesus our Lord."*

I think this verse says it all about how much Christ loves us, no matter what we have done or will ever do; His love surpasses all those things. We need to learn to receive this love into our hearts simply by praying and asking Him to reveal His love deeper into the chambers of our heart, unlocking all the wrong beliefs and thoughts patterns and replacing them with how much Jesus loves us.

Fear and reverence

The only fear that God requires is that of an awesome reverent fear toward Him. *Psalm 128:1 'Blessed (happy, fortunate, to be envied) is everyone who fears, reveres and worships the Lord, who walks in His ways and lives according to His commandments.'* There are rich promises in the word of God as we live and revere Him with all of our hearts.

> *Proverbs 1:7 "The reverent and worshipful fear of the Lord is*
> *the beginning and the principal and choice part of knowledge*
> *(its starting point and its essence) but fools despise skilful and*
> *godly Wisdom, instruction and discipline."*

To fear the Lord is to receive wisdom and understanding and to desire to live right before God. However we cannot obtain our own right living without Christ. He is our righteousness and we cannot be right without His saving grace in our lives. By accepting Jesus into our hearts we choose to follow after His example of living and pattern our lives after

Him. To fear the Lord is when we desire to serve and to please Him, but not in our own strength. It's through the power of the Holy Spirit and His wisdom in our lives. The new nature in us desires to please and live for God, but in our flesh we all make mistakes, this is where we do not have to be afraid of God because He loves us and always forgives us when we are truly repentant in our hearts.

Heart not Works

It's not a matter of works of flesh striving; it's a matter of our true honour in our hearts for God. David was a man who loved God with all of His heart and deeply desired to live for God and to honour Him, but he fell into sin and made terrible mistakes. However, his repentant heart brought him back to a right relationship with God (Psalm 51).

We too can choose this life of love and honour before God and those in authority over our lives. This reverent fear of the Lord keeps us in right living and from straying away off the path He has for us. We are to trust and acknowledge the Lord in every area of our lives. God knows what's best for us. But it's not about living in fear of God or being afraid of Him.

> *Proverbs 3:5, 6 "Lean on, trust in and be confident in the Lord with all your heart and mind and do not rely on your own insight or understanding. In all your ways acknowledge Him and he will direct and make straight and plain your path. Be not wise in your own eyes; reverently fear and worship the Lord and turn entirely away from evil."*

This is a healthy fear of the Lord. He is awesome and mighty, God is holy, and the Bible describes Him as a consuming fire (Hebrews 12:29). But we can draw near to Him, because He is our Heavenly Father and through His Son Jesus He has made a way for us to come close (Hebrews 10:19, 20).

No matter what my children do I don't want them to be afraid of me, I want them to come to me because I love them so much. This is how we are to draw near to God as our Father and Saviour. Even though we may have a reverential fear (respect) we can still draw near no matter what we have done, He loves us and will forgive us.

I used to be afraid of God rather than fear and honour Him. I thought He was always unhappy with me and disapproved of me, especially when I made a mistake or sinned. I felt as though He was waiting for me to make mistakes and it seemed that I did each day. Even in all my works and striving I felt I wasn't pleasing to Him. **My view of God was distorted through fear.** I knew He forgave when I confessed my sins, but I still tried to prove to Him through my works that I would be good. This brought me into a continual spiral of striving and not really accepting His forgiveness and mercy straight away. I had trouble forgiving myself and would beat myself up feeling really bad for days. Fear, condemnation, guilt and unworthiness ruled my thoughts and my heart most of the time.

> *God has not given me a spirit of fear, but of love power and a sound peaceful mind.*

I have since learned to receive His love and forgiveness straight away. He does not stay angry with me; His mercies are new every morning. Now when I make a mistake, I am more able to move on with my life, embraced by His love for me. I don't have to continue in my own works, but in obedience and grace. God is not sitting in heaven with a big four—by-two lump of wood waiting to hit us over the head for our mistakes (This is how I had pictured God as an adolescent).

Because fear brings with it a sense of punishment, we can mistakenly view God as a punishing angry God. Even if our earthly fathers or parents were like this, God is not. He may get angry, but His anger is but for a moment. His mercy and love is from everlasting to everlasting (Psalm 103:10).

To stop living in the wrong fear of God, we must see Him through Truth. His love and grace are there for us even when we fail to do everything right. We have right standing with Him because of the blood of Jesus— He makes us righteous. There is no other way to please the Father, not in our own works, or perfection but in who He is and what He has done for us. James 4:6-8 says to humble ourselves under the mighty hand of God and he will give grace to the humble. **We are saved by grace not our own works! Ephesians 2:8-10—this is the best news any of us could receive.**

Another way of seeing God is to see Him as a big daddy that just longs to hold us in his arms and embrace us as his children. The Bible calls Him Abba Father. Even if you haven't had a father in the natural who nurtured you, God is wanting and waiting to be that father who carefully watches over your life. The Word of God tells us that when you call on Him, He will answer. Remember, He first loved us. Don't allow fear to rob you of a loving relationship with God, for He has made a way for us to draw near through His son Jesus Christ.

If you want freedom from living under fear, release your cares to God once and for all through prayer and begin to put the Word into your heart by speaking it out and meditating on what it says about you and about whom God is. "God has not given me a spirit of fear, but of love, power and a sound peaceful mind!" (2 Timothy 1:7) **God's Nature is Love – Not fear!**

Things changed for me when I would speak the Word of God and confess the scriptures over and over until they became the way I thought and believed. I eliminated the lies and replaced them with the Truth in God's Word.

When you come to know someone well, you build a relationship and trust is established in that relationship. This is what we are doing through the Word of God and in our relationship with Him as we rely on His Word.

Man will let you down, but God will never disappoint us (Romans 5:5) and His love never fails (1 Corinthians 13). I want to encourage you that no matter what your situation, God can be trusted with your heart. When we come to know God's plan we come to understand it is a good plan and not for evil, we have a future and a hope in Him (Jeremiah 29:11).

Trusting God with our dreams

(Genesis 35 & 37:13-24) Joseph had a dream! His dream nearly cost him his life. He had shared his dream with his brothers and they became jealous of him. They didn't understand the meaning of his dream. As a result, Joseph was thrown into a pit by his own brothers, betrayed by them, and then sold into slavery. With his family against him, it seemed all hope was lost. What was to become of his life now? God had a plan for this young man's life, he had a dream in his heart and this was just the beginning. Sometimes things seem to go in the opposite direction to what we think they should. This is how it was for Joseph.

In the years that followed the dream unfolded, not without many challenges and trials, he was tested and tempted, betrayed, set up, imprisoned, yet through it all he trusted that God would bring him through. This is an amazing story of how Joseph totally trusted God's hand in and through every season of his life even when man messed it up for him. God ensured it all turned out for His good.

God can be trusted to take care of our hearts, He will never leave us or forsake us—His promise is to keep us and not let us slip.

> *John 14:27-30 "Peace I leave with you; my own peace I now give and bequeath to you. Not as the world gives do I give to you.*
>
> *Do not let your hearts be troubled neither let them be afraid. (Stop allowing yourselves to be agitated and disturbed; and do not permit yourselves to be fearful and intimidated and cowardly and unsettled).Verse 30 I will not talk with you much longer for the prince (the evil genius, ruler) of the world is coming. And he has no claim on Me. (He has nothing in common with me; there is nothing in me that belongs to him, and he has no power over me.)"*

By us putting the truth on the inside of us we will be able to exude complete authority and power over the evil ruler of this world. Be empowered by the Word of God today and His authority.

Start building today in your minds and hearts new strongholds of truth and life. The Word is filled with truth and life that bring freedom and healing. **Start living today without fear!**

Philippians 4:6-7

Do not fret or have any anxiety about anything, but in every circumstance *and* in everything, by prayer and petition (definite requests), with thanksgiving, continue to make your wants known to God. And God's peace [shall be yours, that tranquil state of a soul assured of its salvation through Christ, and so fearing nothing from God and being content with its earthly lot of whatever sort that is, that peace] which transcends all understanding shall garrison *and* mount guard over your hearts and minds in Christ Jesus.

Here are a couple of simple ways to renew your mind and fill your life with peace, love and joy in the Lord.

*Play some praise and worship music while you pray, sleep, or just spend time at home listening to it, filling the atmosphere with faith.

*Listen to teaching tapes on faith and love to filter the Word into your heart.

Things to remember:

1. Fear is a dream killer; it will stop you from going forward. It will cause you to doubt and shrink back from what God has called you to do. So go ahead and do it afraid anyway.
2. "What if's 'bring confusion they are not from God, He is Yes and Amen. We have to stop reasoning these kinds of questions in our minds.
3. Love is the greatest gift of all; Perfect love casts out all fear! 1 John 4:18, 19. Get grounded in God's love.
4. The only fear we are to have of God is the reverent worshipful fear of the Lord. Proverbs 1:7 Psalm 128:1.

5. Love takes risks—it trusts God even when our trust in others has been broken. *Trusting God with our dreams / Joseph's story Genesis 37:13-24.*

6. FEAR NOT! Isaiah 41:13 says, 'For I the Lord your God hold your right hand. I am the Lord who says to you fear not; for I will help you.'

7. The spirit of fear is not from God—Don't accept it in your life. *2 Timothy 1:6,7*

Just Believe

I've got to come to you in faith
Trust and believe in everything you say
I've got to come to you in faith
Hold onto every word spoken and do what you said

I'm not doubting in my head, but trusting with my heart in You holding
onto the truth
And every word that's spoken You breathe Your life in me
That I can overcome if only I just believe
In You

Facing all my fears and chasing them away
As I stand on Your word I'll trust and obey
And on this rock on which I stand solid there's no sinking sand I put my
hope in You—forever in You

© Paula Connelly 2005 words and music

'Enter His rest in our hearts.'

CHAPTER FIVE

RESTING IN GOD

~Busyness~

*A*re you stressed, burnt out, anxious and worried about your life? Jesus says, "Come to me all you who are heavy laden and burdened and I will give you rest" (Matthew 11:28-30).

I never really knew how stressed I was about life and how low on fuel I was for that matter, because I had been running in the fast lane for too long, until that moment when physically my body couldn't go anymore, I was forced to rest.

Have you noticed how busy everyone is? Moving in the fast lane is the way of life. You just have to ask people, "How are you" and they will say, "Busy!" It's as though being busy makes us important or useful, but if we evaluate our busyness are we busy doing what's really important with our lives? Are we being fruitful with our lives, producers of the harvest? We have to ask ourselves is what I am doing producing everlasting fruit, am I doing the will of God, living in His purpose and plan?

In this part of my journey as I was laid up in bed, God was revealing to me the importance of rest. At first resting seemed like a complete waste of time, but I hadn't learned how to rest because doing was the life style I had only known. Before all of this happened to me I didn't know how to sit still for long, I was always restless and doing something. Sometimes the only way to learn to rest is when you are forced to; this was unfortunately the way I learned to rest. Only now as I have journeyed through this do I understand the importance of this four-letter word that we don't seem to get enough of. I can honestly say this is one of the most important lessons I have learned about life and about walking by faith and I am constantly reminding myself to live in this truth when I get busy again.

Rest begins within the heart

This kind of rest is not just about taking a holiday or a few days off here and there. The kind of rest I'm talking about is more about having a deep sense of rest within our hearts that keeps and sustains our lives every day. It's a rest that enables our hearts to be still and know that He is God and we are not, that He will carry our cares, worries and burdens as we allow Him to. So you can take a deep breath and just trust God.

When Jesus carried the cross, it was symbolic of Him carrying our burdens for us. He took them away so we could come to Him and learn to rest in Him. This kind of rest within our hearts pertains to the confidence we hold in God our Father, it's saying no matter what happens in my life, or what troubles, obstacles, dreams I have to conquer, He holds my life in His hands, God is in control.

It is well with my soul!

I love the story of the woman in 2 Kings 4:18—26 who conceived a son after many years of being barren. However the son, now a young boy, went out into the fields with his father and became ill and suddenly died. The woman saddled a donkey and went on her way to the man of God, the prophet Elisha, whom she trusted to sort out this dreadful situation and raise her son back to life. In her darkest hour when her son had died, she did not lose hope and she spoke with confidence, 'It is well with my soul' in the midst of this tragedy.

Can we honestly say today, no matter what is happening in our lives, in the depth of our hearts, 'It is well with my soul'? This speaks volumes to me about this woman's confidence in God, about her undeniable trust in what God was able to do for her no matter what her situation or the outcome. It is under the grace of God that we can remain free from striving, and say,' it is well with my soul,' purely because of all the Lord has done.

> *Matthew 11:28—30 "Come to me, all you who labour and are heavy-laden and overburdened and I will cause you to rest. (I will ease and relieve and refresh your souls). Take my yoke upon you and learn of me, for I am gentle meek and humble (lowly) in heart, and you will find rest (relief and ease and refreshment and recreation and blessed quiet for your souls). For my yoke is wholesome (useful, good, not harsh, hard, sharp or pressing but comfortable gracious and pleasant) and my burden is light easy to be borne."*

"Come to Me", says Jesus, "and I will give you rest." This is a simple act of our will and through prayer we can come and cast all of our cares upon the Lord who cares for us affectionately. We can do this daily and we can know He hears us.

Even in all of my striving for my goals and dreams I had to learn to trust God and rest in Him that He would bring them to pass, as He promised in His Word (Psalm 37).

I believe that He will do it, as I commit it all over to Him. No amount of worrying or stressing will make it happen any easier or faster. It's truly a matter of saying I give them all to God and I trust that He will guide me and direct my path, so that it will be well with my soul.

In Psalm 37 we see some important keys to live by in handing our cares to the Lord and finding rest for our souls.

> *Psalm 37:3, 4, 5 & 7*
>
> *V3 Trust (lean on rely on, and be confident) in the Lord and do good; so shall you dwell in the land and feed surely on His faithfulness, and truly you shall be fed.*
>
> *V4 Delight yourself also in the Lord and He will give you the desires and secret petitions of your heart.*
>
> *V5 Commit your way to the Lord (roll repose each care of your load on Him) trust, (lean on, rely on, and be confident) also in Him and He will bring it to pass.*
>
> *V7 be still and rest in the Lord wait for Him and patiently lean yourself upon Him.*

Is God in a hurry?

Our ways and our thoughts are not God's, His ways are higher and His thoughts are higher than ours. A day to Him is as a thousand years, we can't even fathom what this looks like. Our times are in His hands. We can only entrust each day to Him and be careful to follow and listen to His voice in leading us day by day.

> *There is a deeper understanding of rest that is found . . . within the heart that trusts God.*

It was interesting to note during this time of recovery that I found myself observing the busyness of my life, family and others around me. It seemed everyone was in a rush; this was the first time I really noticed it simply because I had been right in there with them. It was like watching ants running about, who knows where they are going and what they are doing, but it looks important.

All of us with our busy agendas from morning to night, day after day, week after week diligently working and striving. Ever noticed the years are going by very quickly? Maybe it's because we are all rushing around madly! I was glad to get out of the fast lane and pull over for a while. It gave me a whole new perspective on resting in my life and for my family. We can learn a whole new lifestyle and the value of adding rest to our lives if we just pull up a bit and observe our lives. I can hear people saying now how am I going to make the time for that? It's a matter of the heart; it's matter of obedience in listening for God's wisdom in our lives, pulling over when we need to, and in finding rest in our hearts from all fear. As I have said in the previous chapter, sometimes we can be driven for all the wrong reasons.

It seems our Western culture has been wired with this lifestyle of busyness. Many people in our society work seven days a week to make ends meet, ten to twelve hours a day. In most families both parents are working. With most people affected by petrol rises, interest rises and inflation, families can struggle to stay ahead or make ends meet. The other factor stealing rest from our lives is that we can end up with so much on our plates that there never seems to be enough time in the day to get everything done. Other cultures have a siesta, but in our western society the busier you are the further you will go in life. What's driving us? What's our motivation? A better lifestyle? It seems we are just getting more and more busy and stressed out and many of us are experiencing illness and anxiety because of it all.

I am not saying don't work hard to get somewhere in life, I know it takes hard work and effort to accomplish great things, but we all need balance in our lives and this requires time out for rest, recreation and restoration of our souls. It takes wisdom and listening to the Lord when He calls us to draw aside with Him.

There is a deeper understanding of rest that is found within the heart that trusts God. The rest within the heart is not just about having an annual holiday; this is a rest we enter through trusting and believing God. It's about having faith in Him and believing He knows what's best for us in our lives. By this we can enter into an eternal rest within our hearts, knowing **He has the whole of our life in His hands** (Hebrews 4:1).

Life is not just about working and striving or keeping up with the Jones' or climbing the ladders of success for that matter, there is so much more to enjoying and having fulfilment in our lives. No one gets to the end of their life and says, 'I wish I had more time at the office!' We need to find God's purpose in our lives and in these we find total fulfilment. Jesus only did that which the father spoke to Him about (John 12:49 & 50, John 14:10).

The Word of God tells us we are citizens of heaven, co-heirs with Christ, with access to the Kingdom of God, that's the realm of faith. Our trust is in our Heavenly Father

> *Trying, instead of trusting, makes for a life of striving and stress.*

and through Jesus we live and move and have our being. We are not to pattern our lives after those of this world. However, it can be so easy to get so caught up in all the cares of this world that we miss the true rest God has for us. By putting Him first the rest will follow (Matthew 6:33).

The physical breakdown I experienced was a big wake up call for me. It helped me to stop stressing and striving, and to learn a new way in doing life and making sure I had rest in my life and in my heart. I hadn't known what the word rest meant. I thought if you sat down for too long, you were wasting time and there was no time to waste. In fact I would feel guilty if I sat for too long and rested.

As I have already mentioned the world around us is full of unrest, turmoil and distress, or stress for that matter. Stress is a major health epidemic in today's society with blood pressure, heart disease, strokes, worry, anxiety, and depression often being the end result, to the point of blocking up our hospital system.

Trying, instead of trusting, makes for a life of striving and stress. Sometimes what we think will satisfy us only ends up making us tired, empty hearted and empty handed. One thing for sure, we all have choices to make and those choices will determine our level of joy and peace. One thing to ask ourselves is: even if I have all the riches in the world, do I have rest within my heart? What are we in pursuit of true happiness, peace and joy that comes from God or from the materialistic lifestyle the world has on offer?

There is a way to achieve success, financial freedom, and a lifestyle of peace. It's through the wisdom of God. There is also wisdom in knowing when to chase something down, when to slow down and when to rest and trust in God for those benefits and blessings He has for us. There is a time to build, a time to rest, a time to sow and a time to reap. There is a time and season for everything under the sun (Ecclesiastes 3). The blessings of God include prosperity of the soul, mind and the body. In every way God wants us to prosper.

> *3 John 2 says "Beloved, I pray that you may prosper in every way and (that your body) may keep well, even as (I Know) your soul keeps well and prospers."*

Time is precious. It's one of those things in life we cannot take for granted. Take the time to build relationships, time to plan things properly, time to be quiet and still, as we make some time to prepare, plan and to pray, God reveals a better way for us to go about our lives. His ways are higher than ours; His thoughts are higher than ours (Isaiah 55:8, 9).

How did God do it all?
The great and mighty God of the Universe worked and rested? Here we see God making the earth and all creation, how did He manage it all?

> *Genesis 2: 1-3 "Thus the heavens and the earth were finished, and all the host of them. And on the seventh day God ended His work, which He had done, and He rested on the seventh day from all His work, which He had done. And God blessed (spoke good of) the seventh day, set it apart as His own, and hallowed it, because on it God rested from all His work which He had created and done."*

When God completed His masterpiece, He saw all that He had done. He approved of it, and finally on the seventh day He rested from all His work. Even God needed to rest! He made this day special, holy, separated unto Him because He knew we would need it just as much as He did. This seventh day of rest spoken of in the Old Testament was called the

Sabbath day. A day to draw aside and rest, it was a holy day unto the Lord. Today this Sabbath day is written upon our hearts. It's not necessarily a Sunday or Saturday, although in our Western society these are the noted days off to rest, relax, attend church, and prepare for the rest of the week.

We all need to rest from our labours, have rest in our souls, rest from activity and pressure. There is a satisfaction of working hard, achieving great results and resting after we have worked so hard, enjoying the fruit of our labour. **Rest is a gift from God**. But there is another kind of rest we need to enter. It's the rest we enter through believing and trusting in our hearts. We don't see God striving to make the earth and all that was in it. He commissioned Adam and Eve to take dominion, be fruitful and multiply in the earth. You don't read in the Bible about Adam complaining in the beginning, of all the stress he was under. Sounds like he was just strolling along and enjoying the whole experience of the garden, something most of us would like.

It wasn't until they entered sin and disobedience that turmoil and stress came into the picture. Through their disobedience and sin, the whole of mankind came under this same curse. But in and through Jesus Christ we are freed from the curse, so it's up to us to accept and receive this by faith and to enter it by obedience.

Rest requires our obedience

In Hebrews chapter 3, we see that through disobedience some did not enter the rest God had provided for them. The Israelites, who did not trust or believe God, did not cross over the Jordan because of their hardened unbelieving hearts and in their disobedience, did not enter the rest of God, which was the full promise He had for them.

Rest is a gift from God. Because of their unbelief and hardness of heart they missed what God was saying and doing. Times of wilderness can be trying and often we can become offended at God if the things we are believing for don't come to pass in our timing. Safe to say wilderness times can either harden us and hinder our faith walk or we can learn from them and trust God in the midst of them whether or not we understand His way of doing.

The wilderness can seem empty and a dry place to be in, but in these times if we open our hearts to God and say I will trust you Lord, He will reveal what we need for those times of testing.

The Israelites simply did not trust or believe all that He had for them, they thought they knew better, they decided to camp on the safe side and therefore did not enter into all He had promised for them. But for those who will hear His voice, today that eternal rest is still available to take hold of (Hebrews 4:1-3). We enter the rest by believing God and putting our trust in His word for us.

Rest and faith go hand in hand. When we trust God we enter His rest, because we are simply not striving any longer in our fears or unbelief. It's a good thing to check if you have no rest or peace in your heart. Are you in unbelief or fear? Are you believing the promises of God?

> *Hebrews 4:1 "Therefore while the promise of entering His rest still holds and is offered (today), let us be afraid (to distrust it), lest any of you should think he has come too late and has come short of (reaching) it."*

When God says to rest then let us enter that rest, by trusting in Him. At times we need to just draw aside to hear what He is saying in our hearts about our lives. God doesn't appear to be rushing around in the heavenly realm putting a whole lot of pressure on us to get things done; we put these expectations on ourselves.

This condition of rest within our hearts eliminates our cares, fears, anxieties, worry and all the things that trouble our hearts. Rest from our own works of the flesh and rest from striving in our own strength. As we release our cares to Him, **He cares for us and he lifts the burdens from our hearts.** Often if we are striving in our own fleshy ways we will only have a lot of frustration and anger, this also is a good sign to check if you are in not entering the rest of God. Cease the striving in your own strength, pull back and sit quietly to listen for the Holy Spirit to speak. This is where daily prayer is the greatest gift to us and in our relationship with God. It's about listening to Him and sharing our hearts with God (not just us talking, shouting and petitioning . . . but listening).

I read a book called, *Too busy not to pray* by Bill Hybels. It became evident that finding the time amongst our busyness was the problem.

I guess the thing I have learned the most about this time of rest is how to enter it within my own heart, not striving for things in my own strength, and not being anxious about my life, but to stop and be still and put my trust in the Word of God—learning to live in today not tomorrow (Matthew 6:25-34).

> *Put time with God first and everything else will flow.*

Always worrying about tomorrow brings great amounts of stress to our lives for today. Whenever I have caught myself worrying, I remind myself—today is all I have to deal with. Today God is with me, today I can make decisions with the Holy Spirit as my guide, today I can cast my cares, and today is all I have, right now. There is a position of rest we can all enter and in doing so we will be a whole lot more productive. Put time with God first and everything else will flow. That's why He says, today if you hear His voice. When we hear His voice it stills any other voice or any questions in our minds.

Mary and Martha habits

The difference between being a Mary and Martha in Luke 10: 39-42 was one knew how to sit and listen while the other was busy with many tasks. Jesus brings a clear perspective on the best position for us to be seated. He himself says Mary chose the better position sitting at His feet. Wow that's a biggy for some of us doers to learn . . . Chill out!

I used to be a Martha, always busy and doing things, but I learned that taking time to sit at the feet of Jesus in prayer, being still, is far more beneficial. Putting this time with Jesus first calms all our anxieties and gives us peace for today. Instead of getting up and rushing off to work, get up that little bit earlier just to have this time with Jesus and bring peace and rest into our hearts before the day even gets started. Even getting out of bed, we can be conscious to think and say, 'God you are with me today and I will remain in you.'

It's an attitude of 'apart from God I can do nothing' (John 15:5) so I won't leave the house without this decision in my heart. I want to take Jesus into my whole day and into my heart all day long I am conscious of the Holy Spirit who is there to guide and help me in everything (John 14:16, 17, 18).

Jesus' response to Martha about Mary
"There is need of only one or but a few things. Mary has chosen the good portion (that which is to her advantage) which shall not be taken away from her."

Mary chose to sit at Jesus feet, to be still and quiet and to listen for his voice. Resting in God requires us to stop and be still in our hearts. We can do this even if we are busy; it's an attitude of the heart, always to be tuning in and listening for God.

It also requires us to stop the rushing and hurrying, thinking we can't stop for a moment and just simply quiet our hearts to hear His voice. This takes practise but once you get into the habit it will revolutionise your life.

I have noticed two types of people that don't rush: babies and the elderly people. Babies rely and depend on their parents for everything. The elderly have learned to slow down and take life as it comes; they also know they haven't got much time left, so they treasure what they have. We don't have control over our birth or our death, but we do have control over the life we live in between.

We can learn to stop and smell the roses and take each day as it comes and value it for what it brings. Steal away the precious moments, don't miss them just because you are in a hurry.

Rest, Faith, and Trust
Another good example of resting in God is in the story of 1 Kings 19:12-13. Elijah is hiding in the rock. Here, he hears the gentle small voice of

the Lord. He had been running hard and was very weary (1Kings 19). All of a sudden he positions himself to hearing God's voice but it was in the silence he heard it.

When we rest, we draw aside to hear God's voice speak to our hearts. When we are anxious and worried with our minds overly busy and overloaded we may find it difficult to hear God's voice. I was forever like this, coming up with solutions, I needed to have the answers and I spent most of my time trying to work everything out instead of being still and listening quietly for the voice of God in my heart. While I was in this physical state of rest, due to my chronic fatigue, I was beginning to understand that the physical rest had more to do with my heart and what was going on inside of me. I began to understand that the **rest came as I listened and obeyed.**

Faith is trusting God, even when we can't see our way through, we put our confidence in His ability, not our own understanding. A good example is when we give our tithe and offerings to God, we are saying: "You are my source and my supplier; I put my trust in You." Therefore in our giving we can enter the rest of God that He will do what we cannot do. He will supply all of our needs as we put our trust in Him.

Graeme and I have done this ever since we became Christians and understood this as an act of our faith and trust in God. Even through the toughest times, we have never gone without God's blessing and

> *"Be still and know that I am God."*
> *-Psalm 46:10*

provision in our lives. We can enter the rest because we have obeyed, but by not obeying our hearts become weighed down and heavy and we cannot enter the rest God has for us. You see we have our part to play by this faith is activated. Faith without works is dead. **But remember faith rests and faith trusts.**

It's the super plus the natural, God and man together. God works through our obedience and in this He is able to bring to pass what He says in His word. Our faith in action produces the supernatural powers of God in our lives. Our part is to walk by faith and be doers of the word not just hearers only.

When we put our faith and trust in God we are saying He is our provider. Therefore, we can enter the rest in our hearts and be confident that He will provide what we need. No matter what is going on outside of your world we can choose to stay calm and peaceful on the inside of our lives. When we cooperate with God's plans we enter the rest of God. A good heart check, if you don't have rest and peace, is to ask yourself, "Have I done what God asked me to do?"

Laying everything down

As I had to lay down all my works at this time for my healing to take place, I had to become obedient to this plan. I began to see this principal of **resting = faith**. Everything in me wanted to keep striving, but I had to give in to laying things down for a while and trust God to work things out in my heart. While I did this I entered that place of rest. I began to see things quite differently and hear God's voice a whole lot more clearly.

He had a better plan and bigger plan, it was only through this precious time that I entered the rest that I began to see it. I had always been the type of person who was always in a rush; everything had to happen now.

My parents used to nickname me "the hurricane". I was always striving and hurrying to get somewhere. I have learnt to stop and take breaks and draw aside as a regular part of my day and week. This new way of living brings such peace that it's now something I couldn't do without. Living in the Kingdom of God is about love, joy and peace and when we are reliant on Him for His strength we should not get burnt out. **In fact, when we rely and depend on Jesus, He stretches our capacities even further to doing things we never thought possible.**

I am doing more now than I was before, but I am doing it out of a heart that is trusting and resting in Him. If it's not time for something I just wait in prayer and get on with what I have at hand, without getting anxious about it. Once upon a time if something didn't get done straight away I would get very frustrated and begin to push for it, (in my own strength) until I was worn out.

Listening for His voice, backing off when we need to and being still, are all part of living a life of obedience. We are not to push doors open but wait for God to give us the direction of when to step forward into those doors. Yes, there are times we need to press in through prayer and that is exactly how things will get done in the Spirit first, then in the natural. Faith is believing that what you pray will come to pass! It's when we push in our own strength we end up with trouble in our hearts and minds and no peace.

Isaiah 40:31 "But those who wait for the lord (who expect, look for, and hope in Him) shall change and renew their strength and power; they shall lift their wings and mount up close to God as eagles (mount up to the sun) l they shall run and not be weary, they shall walk and not faint or become tired."

I love this verse in Isaiah 40; it speaks of us soaring on the wings of an eagle, not striving within ourselves, but in His strength and power mounting up closer to God.

Anxiety is the killer of rest. Being anxious and worried about tomorrow never releases us to live in peace for today. Matthew 6:33 says that tomorrow has enough cares of its own. Today is all that really matters. **Focus on today, pray and prepare for tomorrow but don't allow worry to enter your heart.** Just live in today and anxiety will leave your heart.

Becoming a woman of quiet confidence.
'But let it be the inward adorning and beauty of the hidden person of the heart, with the incorruptible and unfading charm of a gentle and peaceful spirit, which [is not anxious or wrought up, but] is very precious in the sight of God.' 1 Peter 3:4

Here in this passage it describes the life of a woman who trusts in God. She is not fretting, fearing or being anxious about her life or family. She has an inner peace because her confidence is in the Lord. This is such a wonderful key as wives, mothers, women of God, to just allow this quietness and stillness to guide us in our hearts.

The Grace of God

The grace of God has been poured out into our life to enable us to live in and through God's strength. It's through His saving grace and ability we can do all things through Christ. Not in our own striving, or boasting, or trying to achieve salvation through our own works of the flesh. We are simply saved by grace through the Lord Jesus Christ, it is a free gift from God (Ephesians 2:8-10)

> *James 4:6 "But He gives us more and more grace (power of the Holy Spirit, to meet this evil tendency and all others fully), That is why He says, God sets himself against the proud and haughty, but gives grace (continually) to the lowly (those who are humble enough to receive it)."*

As we humble ourselves under the mighty hand of God and say in our hearts, "I can't live without You God and Your grace in my life".

He comes and pours more and more of His grace and ability into our lives and reveals His way of living through us. It's an act of our will to surrender all to Jesus and to stop trying and start trusting Him with our hearts. Humility is knowing that God is greater and for us not to become too big in our own eyes. **The bottom line is: we cannot do all we need to and be empowered, without relying on His grace in our lives.**

I can remember sitting at my piano in the year 2000 being very unwell and wanting desperately to be healed. As I just worshipped and went to God, the words of a song came to me. I knew God was telling me to trust Him and to stop fearing, but I needed to believe in my heart and stop doubting in my mind that God had a plan for me. The song that came out at the time was "Just Believe." Even as simple as it sounds sometimes we find it so difficult. But believing accomplishes more than worrying!

Let go and let God be God!

When it comes to faith, we need to listen first to our hearts. Most often we only listen to our minds and the problem with that is, we can overthink and reason away our faith, doubt begins to creep in. We can reason and question until we are in fear and worry only to invite confusion into our lives, when our hearts are telling us to let go and trust God. He's the one who will do the impossible; He will do what we cannot do. He is encouraging us to trust ourselves, our hopes, dreams, bodies, needs to him, but our minds continue to try and figure out how God will do it.

Let go of fear, let go of reasoning in your mind, let go of trying to work everything out. You might say then "what do I do?" Pray, be still and know He is God. He will do it! He hears our every prayer.

Sometimes when we don't hear God's voice or instruction in our hearts straight away, we think we have to get on and do something, but all we need to do is keep being faithful, keep relying on Him and continue to listen for His voice without being anxious. We do our part and God does His, sometimes our part is in just trusting Him to come through. We can only do what God instructs us otherwise we will end up in the works of the flesh. At other times we need to step out to find out which direction to go in. If we lose peace, then we can step back and wait for God to bring peace into that situation once again. He will always reveal the way to go by His peace.

Through this journey of being healed it was impressed on my heart to let everything go that I had been doing at the church. I had been the worship pastor for over ten years and I thought I would be forever. I knew at this time God was calling me to lay it all down. I was very anxious about doing this for fear of letting people down and losing my call and identity in ministry. I wasn't sure I was even hearing from God.

But I had to make a decision that if I was hearing from God I had to follow through. God reminded me of Genesis 22 about Abraham laying down his son on the altar to sacrifice him. If Abraham could give up his son then I could entrust all my dreams and future to Him. Abraham was a man who knew this principle of letting go and letting God take all his life, his possessions, his family his dreams, everything!

In the beginning of **Genesis 12** God tells Abraham to leave everything— his home, his family, his familiar territory and go to another place. Abraham left everything familiar behind, all that he loved and set out on this journey of faith to the unknown. God had said He would show him where to go, so Abraham trusted God's Word and took the step of faith toward it. No questions asked he just did it on the basis of trust.

Just like Abraham, God was calling me to a new thing. I knew in my heart but my mind was coming up with every reason not to do it. Finally I decided to take this step of faith out of my comfort zone and familiarity and walk toward God's purpose and will for my life. It takes faith, not reasoning to obey God. It takes following peace within our hearts.

My Test

I sought God for months over this decision to let go of everything, tossing and turning on how I would go about it. Worrying what my pastor would say, what would the team do without me, I had been part of everything and now I was to let go of all that I knew and was a part of and used to doing.

I had led the worship team in our church for many years and had established quite a large team at our church; this was a dream in my heart. I felt strongly it was the call of God on my life so letting go of this position was very difficult. It didn't make sense to my natural mind and I was afraid to let go. I was afraid of the future, but I had no rest in my heart until I had laid it down completely. I now know it was a test of my trust.

I had been praying for confirmation through my leaders or someone to show me the way in this. Then, the day came when I was driving home from a meeting and my pastor phoned me to say he needed to see me about my future ministry.

> *In the times of silence I have learnt that God knows all and in trusting Him for His timing, I can stay in peace.*

I went to see him and he told me God had spoken to him and I was to go and start a new ministry and let go of everything I was doing in order to do it. Now that is confirmation! I was still afraid but as I obeyed the rest became clear to me. With much guidance from my leaders and handing things over, which took about a year, I ventured into the ministry I now run, speaking and sharing my testimony in other church congregations. It has been the most amazing time of my life, but it only started as I was willing to let go and trust God with my whole life and I am still learning and leaning on God as I write in this journey called faith.

Faith = believing in Him

Hebrews 11:6, without faith it is impossible to please God. This journey is a journey of faith. For me it was laying things I loved on the altar and allowing God to take them even if it meant I wouldn't use those gifts again. I had to let go and trust them to God and understand that he knew what was best for me at this time in my life. As I have discovered even though for a period of time it seemed all was lost and my dreams were on the shelf, slowly God has brought those things back into my life but in a completely different way. My confidence is now established in Him and I know in my heart I am a different person as a result of letting go and trusting Him for His timing in my life. I have learned to follow peace even when fear was tapping on the door of my mind. As we let go of our ways we enter confidently and peacefully into His ways, which enables us to enter the rest of God and His promises.

I wasn't sure if I would ever sing again, having had a damaged vocal cord, but God has restored my singing and even allowed me to fulfil my long-term dream of making my own album of songs about my journey of healing.

It started with me trusting and believing that I had heard Him, trusting His voice and believing that He would do what He said He would. God is the rewarder of our faith; all we have to do is believe.

All it takes is to just believe!

When they asked him what they must do to see miracles, Jesus told his disciples to only believe. In the book of John, there are 98 times God says only believe (John 6:28-29).

Why is it that at times we find this simple act so difficult? Unbelief crouches in our minds, reasoning and fear, always waiting to steal our faith and our trust in God. Doubts and fears steal our peace and our joy, they bring confusion and confusion leaves no room for peace. We believe with our hearts, faith comes by hearing and hearing by the Word preached. The Word is near you, in your heart, and on your lips (Romans 10:9-17).

We must build our faith in the Word of God and by doing so it extinguishes all doubts and unbelief. Even a little child knows how trust with simple faith. Have you ever seen a little child so happy to just leap off a high bench top into the arms of their parent? No fear. Childlike faith is required in believing and entering God's rest. You cannot enter the rest of God without first trusting in what He says.

To build trust in our relationship with God we must spend time with Him. Like in any relationship, once you know that person you learn to trust them.

In my times of silence I have learnt that God knows all and in trusting Him for His timing, I can stay in peace and continue believing. We can miss out on entering the promises of God if we don't learn that entering the rest of God takes faith and trust.

Don't crowd God out

Busyness doesn't produce fruit. I recall one day sitting in my lounge and quietly listening to music and reading my Bible and the Lord showed me a vision—people like ants running around everywhere, going here and there about their lives, busy with their heads down working but no one was looking up to God. It was as though He was waiting for them to just stop, pause (Selah) and look up to heaven. Instead everyone was too busy to even stop for one moment of praise to God.

> *Enter the rest of God and you enter into His promised land and all that He has for you.*

It was like God was waiting for someone to stop and acknowledge Him not because He was lonely or feeling rejected but because He wants to bestow His love and pour out His blessing and favour upon our lives. He is there waiting to touch us and draw near but no one had time.

I believe this was a picture of how busy and frantic we are as humans, but God waits and longs to have a relationship of love with us. James 4:8 says that as we draw near to Him He draws near to us. We can come close to God.

Resting in God requires us to stop from our labours and to draw aside and come near to God. In these times we will hear from God and find rest for our souls. I believe one of the devil's greatest lies and objectives is to get everyone so busy they haven't got time for God. The devil is the evil ruler of this earth and it is his intention to weary people's lives. Stop, pause and have a Selah with God, it will make all the difference in your life and the way you enter God's rest in your souls.

Matthew 13:14-15 describes that if my people would stop and listen, He would heal their land. Is it possible we are too busy to hear from God? I believe in today's society and in the church this is a major problem. God is speaking to His church; maybe if we took more time to waiting on Him we would see the healings over our nations taking place. However, God is sovereign and He will bring to pass His Word according to His faithfulness.

It's time to stop, pause and listen to God—to enter into His rest that we may hear and see what He has for us in this hour. Worship is one of the keys we enter the rest of God; we will talk about this in the final chapter.

> **PSALM 23**
> The Lord is my Shepherd [to feed, guide, and shield me], I shall not lack. He makes me lie down in [fresh, tender] green pastures; He leads me beside the still *and* restful waters. He refreshes *and* restores my life (myself); He leads me in the paths of righteousness [uprightness and right standing with Him—not for my earning it, but] for His name's sake.
> Yes, though I walk through the [deep, sunless] valley of the shadow of death, I will fear *or* dread no evil, for You are with me; Your rod [to protect] and Your staff [to guide], they comfort me. You prepare a table before me in the presence of my enemies. You anoint my head with oil; my [brimming] cup runs over. Surely *or* only goodness, mercy, *and* unfailing love shall follow me all the days of my life, and through the length of my days the house of the Lord [and His presence] shall be my dwelling place. (Amplified bible)

AT YOUR FEET

Here I am just a little while
At your feet, to worship you, to worship you
Is it enough, if this is all I do,
Just to be with you, to be with you

When all is said and done, there's nothing left to do I lay it all down, to
draw closer, to you,

To worship you, is all I long to do
To worship you,
To worship you, is all I long to do
To worship you.

Here I am, just a little while
At your feet, to worship you, to worship you
All that I am, all that I have
I give my life to you, all to you
* I lay it all down, to draw closer, to you.

© 2005 Paula Connelly (Words & Music)

And the peace of God, which transcends all understanding, will guard your hearts and your minds in Christ Jesus. Philippians 4:7

CHAPTER SIX

IN THE PURSUIT OF PEACE

~A Place of Rest~

We can be in the pursuit of many things, happiness, a certain lifestyle, money or even our healing, but to be in the pursuit of peace is something we should all crave for. We just can't live a full, joy-filled life without the peace of God deep within our hearts.

There is a place of serenity and quiet where all is calm. That place may be found in locations, holiday resorts, a quiet room but the true place of peace I am speaking of is within the person of the Lord Jesus Christ. In His heart for us is His gift of peace.

As we receive of His peace and abide in Him our lives become lives that are calm and peaceful. We choose peace; yes it's a choice to stay in peace no matter what the storms of life bring. God still calms the raging seas! The raging seas we sometimes find ourselves in, or within ourselves. You can be in a difficult situation but still remain in peace or you can allow the trouble to disturb you and lose your peace. If you call on Jesus He will calm the storms and give you peace within, even when everything is out of control.

Jesus is seated at the right hand of the father. His position is sitting down, symbolic of resting. When Jesus hung on the cross, He announced in His final hour, "It is finished". There is nothing more that needed to be done; He conquered sin and death, sickness and disease all at Calvary. He purchased our freedom from all fear, freedom from this world and its sorrows. In and by Him we are made co-heirs with Christ, we too are seated (spiritually) in the heavenly realms. Our position is in Christ.

> **Ephesians 2:6** *"And he raised us up together with Him and made us sit down together (giving us joint seating with Him) in the heavenly sphere (By virtue of our being) in Christ Jesus (the Messiah, the Anointed One)."*

Our peace and our rest are in this position in Christ. He has done all that was required in giving us a full life, all we need to do is enter that rest and peace by believing and receiving all that He has done. It's not about what we can do, but about what He has already done.

Pursue peace
Peace was something I desperately wanted deep in my heart. For so long I had been in turmoil now I absolutely craved this peace.

Psalm 34:14 Depart from evil and do good, seek, inquire for and crave peace and pursue (go after it)!

How desperate are we to have peace, we must crave it like air and go after it like it's all we need. I wanted to silence the negative thoughts and all the reasoning that went on inside my mind and my heart. The only way this happened was as I renewed my mind daily in the Word of God.

I literally spoke the Word out over my life, I wrote Scriptures on paper and hung them on the walls and the fridge, I had to get the Word on the inside of my heart and mind to stay in peace.

> **Isaiah 26:3** *"You will guard him and keep him in perfect and constant peace, whose mind (both its inclination and it character) is stayed on you, because He commits himself to you, leans on you and hopes confidently in you."*

Those whose minds!
It's again a matter of our thinking. What disturbs us often is what we think upon. If you think upon all your cares and worries you most certainly will not have peace, but if you renew your mind in God's Word

and allow it to wash over like water it will refresh and give you peace in your heart and in your mind.

I used to say I needed to get away and find some peace. If only I could go on a holiday, if only I could find peace! **You can't live without peace but neither can you run away to find it.** I have been on many beautiful beaches and watched sunsets and felt peace in that moment, but when I came home from that holiday the unsettling would begin again. The unsettling was in me and in the way I handled things.

I was an aggressive, impatient, attacker of life. What I wanted I wanted now and straight away. I have been working on this area of my life, because my personality is by nature more aggressive, I am learning to replace this with being assertive and patient with others and myself. This has taken time, but I have learnt to stop and think about my reactions and learning to respond in a more peaceful way in my life. You can do the same.

We need to be constantly choosing peace over anxiety and worry. We need to be in pursuit of peace, making it a constant decision in our hearts to remain in the peace of God, no matter what situations may come our way. Again as we search our hearts for what is unsettling us, often we will hear the still small voice of God whisper what we need to address in our lives.

This peace I am talking about is deep within the heart. It's a knowing God is with you, right there beside you, in you and will never leave you.

Peace that calms the inner man
After she received her second kidney transplant and having come close to death on several occasions in her life, my sister described this peace that kept her. She said she just knew God would get her through, and He did. She never complained about the pain or the ongoing treatments and operations she had to go through. Even as I am writing she is encountering her third time with failed kidneys, but she remains stable and fixed under the shadow of the Almighty.

> *Psalm 91 "He who dwells in the secret place of the most high shall remain stable and fixed under the shadow of the Almighty (Whose power no foe can withstand).*
>
> *I will say of the Lord, He is my refuge and my fortress, my God; on Him I lean and rely, and in Him I (confidently) trust."*

This kind of peace within makes us stable and fixed; it enables us to stand in the midst of storms not being tossed about and keeps us immovable on the rock of Jesus Christ. **The Kingdom of God is about righteousness, peace and joy!**

> *Philippians 4:7 "And God's peace shall be yours that tranquil state of a soul assured of its salvation through Christ, and so fearing nothing from God and being content with its earthly lot of whatever sort that is, that peace) which transcends all understanding shall garrison and mount guard over your hearts and minds in Christ Jesus."*

Practice peace

Becoming a peacemaker takes practise, each day we need to decide to stay in peace. Now if you are like me it will take some practise to become a peacemaker. I am the fighting aggressive type, so I had to learn to respond in a whole different way to people and circumstances.

My husband is quite the opposite. If we had a decision to make I would have a million questions and solutions all at once and he would just say that it would work out, and quietly go about his business without seemingly a care. This used to frustrate me because I would think why he isn't acting on it quickly; I have since learned things do always work out in the end. Not saying we should procrastinate and be passive about everything, but we can learn to be patient and stay in peace until we have the answers. My impatience or reasoning would often lead me out of peace.

Strife kills peace and harmony

Allowing inner peace to enter our souls comes from knowing the Lord

For so many years I was an argumentative person, always wanting the last say, or allowing myself to get so upset about things, it would end up in a big screaming match between myself and Graeme. I have had to learn to give up the fight and let go in order to have peace. Graeme would say that I was "crescendo-ing". I would get louder and louder to get my point across. I think for the first ten to fifteen years of our marriage this is how I worked things out. So to undo all those years of strife I have had to work hard on my part to become a peace-maker, not to react in anger and quarrelling, but in taking time to evaluate how I will approach our conversations and discussions, and today we both still continue to work on keeping peace in our marriage.

It's something we have to continually be aware of, we may fail at times, but we must keep getting back on track and allowing the Holy Spirit to help us. Strife has the root of pride behind it and it certainly doesn't care, but wants to win every argument at any cost. On the other hand, humility backs down, is patient, and humbles itself in order to make peace.

I know there are many families living in strife and it is tearing them apart. Recognise strife and its evil; it's not worth ruining our families, marriages or relationships. What I had to weigh up was, did I really need to be so aggressive? Could I communicate more effectively with my husband and children by controlling my temper?

The Bible says be slow to anger. Don't become so angry so quickly and don't harbour anger for hours on end, it will definitely kill your peace (Ephesians 4:26, 27).

We can stay angry for hours on end well into the night and wake up feeling ill because of it, churning away on the inside, or we can decide to deal with it quickly by forgiving that person and ourselves and by humbling ourselves. After a while I have come to realise it's just not worth it.

I have learnt to evaluate why I was getting angry. Was it fear, and most of the time it was or frustration for not getting things done straight away clearly being impatient with others. There is a caution line for anger and strife if we go over it then we are in danger of bringing all kinds of evil into our homes, and this is not God's will for our lives.

Galatians 5:19-20 says that the flesh is opposed to the spirit, if we operate out of the flesh, strife, jealousy, anger, ill temper, selfishness and the like, we will only produce these things, but as we decide to operate out of the fruits of the Holy Spirit, love, joy, peace, patience, goodness, kindness, faithfulness, gentleness, meekness and self control we will produce these in our lives (Galatians 5:22, 23). We choose to operate out of the spirit or out of the flesh; we decide what is going to control us!

We need to decide how we will handle situations before they arise, and decide how we will respond instead of reacting. In our business as builders most years we have had the extremes of being overly busy then overly quiet, it can be so tempting to fret and fear when there is not a lot of work on, but we have learned that in this season we can continue to sow and trust God that He will bring through what we need and He always has. We have had our years of difficulty in business and we have had ours years of reaping, each season reveals our trust and confidence in the Lord. We have decided no matter what season we are in we won't lose our peace about it.

Be still and know that God is God!
Another thing to practise is being still. This is being silent within our hearts. Not fretting, not fearing but saying to our souls, "Be still my soul." Sometimes you have to speak to the soul, the inner man on the inside of you and say, "Be still! I am not going to fret or worry, I am going to wait patiently for the Lord, and He is my helper."

Allowing inner peace to enter our souls comes from knowing the Lord and that He is not a God of fear but love, peace and joy.

How would you like to have perfect peace?
An overly busy mind is not a peaceful mind. There have been days where my mind just wouldn't shut up; my thoughts would be going from one

thing to the next. Sleeplessness and restlessness in our inner man comes from an overly busy mind trying to reason and work everything out instead of trusting them to God. I used to go over and over things until I was literally confused in my mind. I found it hard to make decisions because I was in fear and didn't know which way to go. The only way to capture these thoughts of reasoning is to go to the Word of God and renew our minds.

Renewing our minds renews our hearts, reading and meditating on the Scriptures daily, listening to praise and worship and thinking upon the Lord will ease a troubled heart and mind. In order for us to stay in peace we must **come to know God and His word for our lives**. Through knowing Him we can allow peace to rule us and not our negative thoughts or emotions.

In John 14:27 Jesus tells His disciples to receive his peace not as the world gives, but a peace that is everlasting. We need to learn to be reciprocators of peace, and maintainers of peace. There is enough turmoil going on in the world, Jesus knew the one thing we would need is peace. We each have the opportunity to show the peace that God gives to us and by being a peacemaker we are showing it to others.

God's Kingdom is a government of peace
God's covenant with us is a covenant of peace and a government of peace. Isaiah 9:6-7 says, *For to us a Child is born, to us a Son is given; and the government shall be upon His shoulder, and His Name shall be called Wonderful Counsellor, Mighty God, Everlasting Father Prince of Peace. Of the increase of His government and of peace there shall be no end.*

What an amazing promise for us, that His peace is a government over us that will never end. In fact it will only increase and of peace there shall be no end. In a world with rumours of wars we can have an internal peace within our hearts and minds. We can say the Lord is my peace and He is over me.

Our earthly governments may not bring peace but our heavenly government brings all the peace we need. We can enter into The Lord's promise of peace today as we commit all our hearts, minds and wills to the Lord.

> *'For I know the thoughts and plans that I have for you, says the Lord, thoughts and plans for welfare and peace and not for evil, to give you hope in your final outcome.'*
> *Jeremiah 29:11*

Things to remember about staying in peace:

1. Jesus gives to us peace, not as the world gives (John 14:27).

2. Pursue peace, crave for it, and go after it (Ps 34:14).

3. Keep your mind in peace (Isaiah 26:3).

4. Practice peace with everyone (Romans 12:18).

5. Strife, arguments and pride destroy peace (Galatians 5:17-19).

6. Discover the fruit of the Holy Spirit—love, joy, peace . . .

   (Galatians 5:22, 23).

7. Be still and know God (Psalm 46:10). Isaiah 9:6,7

'Positioned to be in His Presence'

CHAPTER SEVEN

HEART OF WORSHIP

~Worship~

*W*e have established how important it is to have the Word in our hearts daily, but there is another important factor in how we position our lives daily in worship.

Why is worship important to God?
In John 4:23 Jesus says, "A time will come, however indeed it is already here, when the true(genuine) worshippers will worship the Father in spirit and in truth (reality); for the Father is seeking just such people as these as His worshipers. God is spirit (a spiritual being) and those who worship Him must worship Him in spirit and truth (reality)."

In the previous verses Jesus had already told the woman that it's not about a place of worship on this mountain or in this city of Jerusalem, but it's about a people of worship. Those who are true worshippers know and understand who they are worshipping.

> **John 14:6 "I am the Way, the Truth and the Life, no one comes to the father except by (through) Me."**

It's not about religion or tradition but sincere hearts that draw near to God (Hebrews 10:22). It's about our spirits connecting with God's Spirit. As we are born again we come alive to His spirit and the truth that Jesus is the Saviour and the one we are to worship.

This woman at the well knew of God and the Messiah but she didn't know Him in her heart (John 4:25). God wants us to know Him for who He really is. **How we see God will determine how we worship Him.** Growing up as a child I had this picture in my mind of God being this big old father in the heavens. He was far away and untouchable. White beard, glowing brilliant white hair, angels all around His golden throne, this was a picture of God in all His glorious splendour in Heaven.

Another picture of God I often recall is the one in the old movies, where Moses is holding up his staff to the waters, and with the wind blowing in his silver hair and the sound of God's voice coming from heaven; He separates the waters over the red sea. It's a picture of the miraculous and awesomeness of God moving through a man.

> *How we see God will determine how we worship Him.*

I used to love those old movies, they made me feel like God was so big and so amazing and I would be drawn to wanting to know more. It wasn't until I was a teenager that I got the opportunity. My first visit to a Pentecostal, born again believing church was when I was sixteen. I had an encounter with God that was very real and I was born again, but somehow I just wasn't ready to give God my all, so I didn't return until I was 18. In this time I met my husband, Graeme. We got engaged and together attended the same Pentecostal church, *Faith City*, for my mother's water baptism, it was at this event that we both fully committed our lives to Jesus Christ and we have never looked back.

Jesus has truly captured my heart by His amazing love and continues to do so. My view of God has changed from seeing God as a distant Heavenly Being, to a very up, close and personal God and Father who is always with me and in my heart, and Jesus as my Saviour. It's out of this heart transformed by His love and grace that I now understand how to draw near in worship.

All that is within me—is Jesus, His love, His presence and His life.

Love the Lord your God with all your heart and with all your soul and with all your mind (intellect) Matthew 22:37

This key scripture depicts that we are to love Him with everything our hearts, souls, minds our whole being.

Worship is all about our hearts truly connecting in relationship with our God, knowing Him and being known by Him. Seeing Him for who He is. He is great and mighty and able to do anything. Nothing is impossible with God. He is a strong tower; refuge and fortress, those that run into Him are saved. He is merciful and kind, loving and full of grace.

Having an open and honest heart in worship

In the Bible, we see that David's heart was open, honest and sincere in worship. He was willing to be vulnerable before God knowing nothing was hidden from His sight. He poured out his heart to God in troubled times and in the good times. He gave praise in the midst of terrible circumstances; he was totally devoted to God.

> **Psalm 9 "I will praise you, O Lord with my whole heart; I will show forth (recount and tell aloud) all Your marvellous works and wonderful deeds! I will rejoice in You and be in high spirits; I will sing praise to Your name, O most high."**

No matter what happened, he gave praise and adoration to God and he kept his heart before the Lord in worship.

When Jesus is the one we centre and focus upon, He is magnified and all else fades. The mountains in our life get smaller and the troubles in our heart fade away. No matter how you see God, the Bible says He is near and He is in everything.

> **Psalm 19 "The heavens tell of the glory of God. The skies display his marvellous craftsmanship. Day after day they continue to speak; night after night they make him known.**
>
> **They speak without a sound or a word their voice is silent in the skies; yet their message has gone out to all the earth and their words to all the world."**

God can be seen in our surroundings, but He can also be felt and known in our hearts and in our daily lives. His presence is tangible as His love is tangible and real. Just one encounter with God and you are never the same. All we have to do is decide to draw near to Him in our hearts. Call on Him and He will hear you.

The Woman at the Well encounters Jesus (John 4:1-26)

Jesus speaks to a woman at the well about giving her living water that will forever satisfy her thirst. This water of course was a picture of eternal life and satisfaction with Jesus as her Lord and Saviour. Jesus reveals to her the dissatisfaction of her life having had five husbands and being onto her sixth husband. He revealed that something was still missing from her life. Her heart was still searching.

> *The heart of worship is a heart that is satisfied and focuses solely on the person of Jesus Christ.*

I believe He was revealing to her a deeper level of intimacy and love that she couldn't find in a husband. It would only come through a personal relationship with Him as her Saviour. Only Jesus truly satisfies the heart, through His word, His promises and his grace in our lives. We have to ask ourselves: is He the one satisfying us and filling us or is it the world and material things? What do we crave for, Entertainment, money, things? Or a deeper relationship with our God as David did and as this woman at the well was looking for.

We may even start out hungry and desperate for God but once we get on this journey of faith we can become complacent, dry, empty and our need for God has become less than it should be. But as we hunger for Him the hunger will grow and our love and fire for Him will be stirred up again.

Like the woman in the Bible, many are in this exact predicament today in the search for love, acceptance and complete satisfaction. People are in search of an intimate loving relationship that does not disappoint or reject. That can only be found in the person of Jesus Christ because God is love! Jesus came to show us His love on the cross, by giving up His life for us, and in return all He says is if you come to me and believe in me I will love you all your life into eternity. In worship we can draw near and have an intimate up and close and personal relationship with Jesus every day.

We can easily get disillusioned in our relationships and try even in our marriages for our husbands to fill our void but only God can fill it deep within our hearts. In fact it's way too much pressure for our husbands, boyfriends or even friends to be all that we need. As we go to Jesus, He will fill the emptiness with living water.

Time is all we need. Make a heart felt decision to stop being in a hurry and to give time in worship. It's a strong conviction in my heart to encourage people to get back to that place of devotion and adoration before our great and mighty God. This is a decision to position ourselves in worship and devotion at His feet. It's an attitude of the heart that says I will put God first in my life. How long has it been since you had time like this at the feet of Jesus.

I truly believe busyness robs us of this precious time with Jesus. It seems there are always a million things to be done. I have come to understand that God is more interested in us being *with* Him than just doing things *for* Him all of the time.

Like in any relationship you have to spend quality time with that person to really come to know them. Over the years I keep coming back to this one thing, as I spend time with my Saviour, everything else flows. This is my first priority. **Psalm 27:4** describes it likes this saying, *'this one thing have I asked of the Lord, that will I seek'*, as we aim to do this one thing, not ten things, but giving first place to God everything else will flow..

The greatest thing is to know Him and be known by Him.

We can get so busy that this is the last thing we do and if we don't make time, we can grow cold in our hearts. Maintaining a healthy heart full of the love of God comes from being in His presence. There have been times in His presence where I have been so overwhelmed by His love, that I can't speak or move, I just sit quietly taking it all in and tears will begin to roll down my face as I know He is so near. He always pours out His love.

Counting all things but rubbish!

Paul the apostle says in Philippians 3:8 and 9, "I count everything as loss compared to the possession of the priceless privilege (the overwhelming preciousness, the surpassing worth, and supreme advantage) of knowing Christ Jesus my Lord and of progressively becoming more deeply and intimately acquainted with Him (of perceiving and recognizing and understanding Him more fully and clearly.) For this sake I have lost everything and consider it all to be mere rubbish in order that I may win (gain) Christ (the Anointed one). And that I may actually be found and known as in Him."

You see, **the greatest thing is to know Him and be known by Him.** And this is where we need to be positioned in worship as the priority of our lives. To sum it up, it's about our affection and devotion to God. It's how we live and move and have our being in Him. I have found that the more I hunger after God the more I pursue Him, the closer I get.

Staying hungry for Him

As we become desperate enough and search for Him in our hearts we will find Him. Keeping our dependence upon the Lord and not becoming self-reliant is the key.

> *Jeremiah 29:12, 13, 14 "Then you will call upon Me, and you will come and pray to Me, and I will hear and heed you. Then you will seek Me, inquire for, and require Me (as a vital necessity) and find Me when you search for Me with all your heart. I will be found by you, says the Lord."*

The one thing God looks upon is our hearts. Yes He sees all we do, all we are, all we think and say, but when all is said and done on this earth it's our hearts that he is looking for—hearts that are hungry for His presence, with a deep longing for more of Him.

We could misinterpret this need for more things and get caught up in this, but actually God has set eternity in our hearts and this desire for eternity is to be with Him. His original plan was to have a family and to create a relationship with man that was intimate, personal and life long. God gave man everything he needed in the garden and even the joy of walking face to face with God everyday. Adam walked in the cool of the garden talking to God. The one and only God of the universe that everyone on planet earth wonders about, Adam actually walked with Him. They talked, shared and spent time together—man and God.

This is how it is meant to be. **Worship opens the door of our hearts and opens the way to heaven**, giving us full access through all that Jesus Christ has purchased. The way is open for us to enter into His presence in our hearts every day (Hebrews 10: 19, 20).

As a worship pastor I have had the privilege of leading worship in our church and other places, but nothing takes the place of this one thing, my personal time with God. I keep coming back to this one thing: **Our hearts embracing Him and all that He is, our hearts centred and focused on Him.** The giving of our whole hearts is to give our all, our whole being, body, soul, and spirit in pursuit of God.

How hungry are we for God to satisfy us? I know when I am hungry for food I will eat just about anything to satisfy that grumbling hunger. But really how desperate are we for His presence? Knowing our need for God keeps us hungry. Not becoming self-reliant, self-confident, and complacent with the things of God. Keeping our first love for Him is the key.

Here is a picture in the Psalms of David's longing for God:

> *Psalm 42:1, 2 "As the hart pants and longs for the water brooks, so I pant and long for you, O God. My inner self thirsts for God, for the living God. When shall I come and behold the face of God?"*
>
> *Psalm 63:1-8*
>
> *O God, You are my God, earnestly will I seek You; my inner self thirsts for You, my flesh longs and is faint for You, in a dry and weary land where no water is.*
>
> *So I have looked upon You in the sanctuary to see Your power and Your glory. Because Your loving-kindness is better than life, my lips shall praise You. So will I bless You while I live; I will lift up my hands in Your name.*
>
> *My whole being shall be satisfied as with marrow and fatness; and my mouth shall praise You with joyful lips.*
>
> *My whole being follows hard after You and clings closely to You; Your right hand upholds me.*

I realised during my time of rest and recovery how much I had missed being close to God. It's true sometimes the toughest trials in our life draw us closer to God, simply because we are crying out for answers. I know in this time for me I wanted to desperately find God's peace and presence in my life. When we get desperate we usually find what we were looking for.

Through this time God showed me to re-position myself in His presence not just praying and petitioning Him for things but to receive His love and pour out my heart in love for Him. As I surrender my heart in worship I am strengthened in His presence.

Prioritising our devotion

We can be devoted to many things, our family, our jobs, ministry, money, our hobbies, and entertainment but what about our devotion to God our heavenly Father and to Jesus our Saviour who has given us life and salvation.

So much time spent on other things can steal our devotion to God. I am not saying don't be devoted to your family, marriage, children, and work. These are necessary to be devoted to, but there are so many other things that take the place of our devotion and time, we can get so consumed with things and never have time for God. When we give the Lord first place in our lives, everything else falls into alignment with His will for us, the key is in seeking first His kingdom.

I can be so driven by works for example and get so consumed with doing things, that I can become so busy I have no time for God. He just gets put on the end of my list of things. This is where I have had to adjust and prioritise my devotion. Another thing I love doing is going to the movies and just chilling out.

Now this isn't a terrible thing to do, but there have been times when I really felt in my heart to lay this down and spend time with God instead. As I have obeyed, I have been truly blessed in my heart by choosing to be with the Lord instead of being entertained. All it takes is us having a sensitive heart, listening to the Lord. When He calls us in our hearts we should respond with, "Yes Lord I hear you."

Worship renews us in our hearts and minds
In Romans 12:1-3 Paul the apostle urges us to offer our lives as living sacrifices holy and pleasing to God. This means our entire body, mind, emotions and will by laying them down, on the altar. That is, giving up our own ways and surrendering to the will of God. This is pleasing worship to the Lord. Then, we are to be transformed and changed in our thinking, not following in the way of the world. And by doing this we will know the perfect will of God. Worship renews us, in our hearts and minds, when we truly surrender all to Him.

Waiting on God (Isaiah 40:28-31)
Waiting on God is the key to soaring in life—soaring in His strength, mounting up close to God on the wings of an eagle majestically soaring above the clouds to greater heights in Him.

We must keep the Lord first place and all the rest will fall into place.

It takes time to wait. I was not good at this, most of the time I was too impatient to wait on God. One of the keys in worship is taking time to wait on God, to allow Him to speak into our hearts. The key is to wait expectantly, (confidently) and in hope!

Waiting can sometimes seem like forever. There can be frustrations of not doing, not being where we want to be; yet waiting is a part of life's journey. If we don't wait we won't be ready for what's ahead. This has been one of the most important lessons I have come to understand.

To wait is to be still and not to move before your time. Jesus waited; He was the Son of God, but from birth to 30 years of age he was hidden in silence; the silence of waiting, the years on the shelf and the years of preparation. Why wait? God knows when we are ready, He knew when it was time for Jesus to be launched on the world, and He knows when it's time for me and you. We can be in such a hurry.

God was dealing with me in this area of waiting and being patient for his timing. He was also teaching me something most important, that would set me up for the long term. Waiting on the Lord gives us His strength and renews us in Him.

Through waiting on God, I was learning to rely and depend on His way of doing. This meant not moving until God was ready and told me to do so. So I spent time in worship, reading, praying, listening, relaxing and being a good mum and wife, helping at work, but mostly waiting on God. There were days that I felt the pangs of frustration wash over me.

Humility (James 4:6)
God gives more grace to the humble; those who are willing to put themselves under and in submission to God. There is humility in waiting. This means our total dependence is upon Jesus and not our ways. Humility leads us to lean on and depend on Christ—it's saying I am not confident in my own strength or wisdom, but I want God's ways more than my own.

When we think we can do life without him we have stepped into the pride of life. It's subtle, but doing things in our own confidence is not

God's way of doing things. **To be humble is to say I can't do life without relying of Him first.** As we wait upon the Lord our strength shall be renewed like the eagles. And in this we will be able to soar to great heights in Him.

The Power of Praise!

Another important thing about worship is the power of praise in the midst of difficult times. Despite our circumstances, we choose to worship. This is a position of faith in our worship and it establishes God on the throne of our lives.

> **Psalm 34:1 "I will bless the Lord at all times His praise shall continually be in my mouth."**

Not sometimes but at all times. Not complaining, not murmuring but praising Him at all times. A decision of praise and thanksgiving will draw us closer to God and His will in our lives.

Paul and Silas were imprisoned, beaten and chained (Acts 16:23-26). But at the midnight hour they began singing and praying hymns of praise to God. What happened next was powerful! Suddenly there was a great earthquake, so that the very foundation of the prison was shaken; and at once all the doors were opened and everyone's shackles were unfastened! I love this passage; it reveals the power of praise in the midst of trouble. Not only were Paul and Silas free but everyone else in the jail was free.

As we decide to praise Him in the midst of our trials, there is no telling what God will do in our lives and in our families.

Another position of worship in battle is in 2 Chronicles 20, the story of King Jehoshaphat. He was told a great multitude was coming against him to battle. He decided to seek the Lord. It says he set himself to seek the Lord and proclaimed a fast in Judah. In Verse 17 the Lord says to him, *"You shall not need to fight in this battle; take your positions, stand still and see the deliverance of the Lord. King Jehoshaphat bowed his head with his face to the ground, and all Judah and the inhabitants of Jerusalem fell down before the Lord, worshipping Him."*

As the story goes on, the musicians and singers were sent ahead of the army in praise and loud singing, this brought great confusion to the enemy and therefore the enemy slaughtered themselves and Judah won the battle. **Next time the enemy is giving you a hard time just begin to sing and praise the Lord and see the battle won in your life.** Worship takes place when we release all our cares to God and draw near to Him with hearts full of faith, confidence and trust.

Worship and healing

How many people in the Scriptures fell at the feet of Jesus in worship and He healed them all. A few to mention from the Gospels are: the leper, the mad man amongst the tombs, the ruler of the synagogue, and the woman with the issue of blood (Mark 5).

Nothing will change your heart more and heal you more than getting into the presence of God and just worshipping Him for who He is. Not just seeking for healing but the seeking the healer.

As we humbly submit our hearts to Him in worship, he draws near to us. We need to decide: will we be consumed with hearts of worry or hearts of worship? You've heard me say that I spent most of my time in fear, anxiety and worry going around the same mountain of issues, instead of going up the mountain to worship to meet with God. As we worship and position ourselves in His presence it enables God to do what only He can do. Worship establishes our hearts in Him, firmly in faith. We become immovable and full of faith, hope and love as we are fixed upon Him.

Worship changes our perspective and view of God from looking at our mountains to looking at the mountain maker. God! What matters most to God is our hearts in worship. I believe God is calling us into His presence and as we respond He will reveal Himself to us in even greater ways. We just need to re-position ourselves in His presence. It's out of worship that our hearts are truly transformed by His love and grace and we come to Know Him for who He is.

This has been the most important place and position in my life, at His feet in worship.

Psalm 24:6—8 "This is the generation (description) of those who seek Him (who inquire of and for Him), who seek Your face, (O God of) Jacob. Selah (pause and think of that)!

Also [Jesus] told them a parable to the effect that they ought always to pray and not to turn coward (faint, lose heart, and give up). Luke 18:1

CHAPTER EIGHT

NEVER LOSE HEART & NEVER GIVE UP!

~The Power of Prayer~

*T*here is an enemy, the devil, who wants to wear us down to the point that we are weak and tired, sick and distressed. But we are to be aware of this enemy and fight with the sword of the spirit. Our weapons of warfare are not carnal but mighty for the pulling down of strongholds. These weapons we fight with are revealed in the Word of God, through the Holy Spirit and Prayer. Persistence in prayer is a powerful key for each of us to take hold of. (Luke 18:1)

> *1 Peter 5:8 "Be well balanced (temperate, sober of mind), be vigilant and cautious at all times, for that enemy of yours, the devil roams around like a lion roaring (in fierce hunger), seeking someone to seize upon and devour. Withstand him; be firm footed, established, strong, immovable, and determined, knowing that the same sufferings are appointed to your brotherhood (the whole body of Christians) throughout the world."*

One night a miracle occurred.

I remember the night I was completely healed of the stomach problems I had at this time. I was awoken by my daughter crying in pain from a toothache, it was 3 am. I got up with Graeme to attend to her and finding no medicine in the house, we prayed that she would be healed and immediately she went back to sleep. I was also in pain and had been night and day with stomach and bowel problems for over two years. As a result of all the stress the doctors still with no solutions just told me to watch my diet but nothing stopped the pain. I was down to eating salads and not much else as most things caused terrible pain in my stomach for hours. I couldn't enjoy eating meat or drinking milk or sweets because if I did indulge I would end up in so much pain it was unbearable. I had lost a fair bit of weight also because of it and lacked the energy I needed.

This night I just couldn't take it anymore! The pain was unbearable but something rose up on the inside of me and enough was enough! I said to my husband I have had enough of this pain I am going to stay up and pray until I am healed. With that he agreed to stay up with me, the time was 3.30am. We began to pray and cry out to God, speaking out the Word and telling the enemy he had no authority over my life.

By 4.30am my husband went back to bed. I continued and sat on the floor with my Bible in my lap, reading and speaking out the Scriptures while listening to worship music. There was a determination in my heart, I knew this was my night. I wasn't going to give in easily or give up. I made a decision that this was it, no more pain; I was going to be healed. I remember sensing a strength and faith rise up within me like never before.

By 6:00am I fell asleep on the floor for about ten minutes, I awoke and felt no pain in my stomach. I got up and pressed my stomach and felt no pain. Then, I ran down to the kitchen and made myself a hot chocolate with full cream milk, which I could not drink normally.

I drank it and there was no pain. I ran back to our bedroom and told my husband, the pain had gone. I ate breakfast and throughout the next two weeks I had no pain at all. I knew I was healed. I went out for dinner that week and had my first steak in two years, with no pain! This may be small to someone else, but it was a big deal to me.

Suddenly, two weeks later the pain returned I could not believe it. I knew I was healed but all of a sudden it came back with a vengeance. I stood on my balcony crying out to God and asking Him why. I clearly heard His voice saying to me, "Check what you have been thinking upon." I thought about what He was saying and realized that I had been fearing that the pain may come back. I felt the Lord tell me I had allowed fear and unbelief to enter my heart.

I made a decision right there on my balcony to repent and ask the Lord's forgiveness for my unbelief and fear. The pain left me immediately and I have never had it again.

Persistence in prayer

Like the woman in Luke 18 we are called to pray and never give up! **Don't lose heart because you didn't get your answer straight away, keep going.** Get others to pray with you, but be determined to not give up. Press in! Press past the negative doctor's report, the hurts of the past, the pain you feel. Press past fear and negativity and touch Jesus with your faith. Press past what people say or think about you, the fear of man is a snare. We have to go beyond our feelings and put our prayers into faith gear, up and at it. Not by might or power, but by your Spirit, says the Lord (Zechariah 4:6); in other words not in our own strength or arm but by the power of the Holy Spirit. (Romans 8:26-27) Praying in the Spirit is the key. The Spirit makes intercession for us. God knows our needs before we even ask but He still expects us to pray according to His will. **Not in fear or worry, but faith believing that what you pray you will receive.**

Again, the woman in Mark 5:25-34 with the issue of blood, she decided if she could touch Him she would be healed. *Verse 28, "for she kept saying, 'if I only touch His garments, I shall be restored to health.'"*

Another illustration is the blind man in Luke 18:35-42. He called and shouted out until Jesus heard him, and stopped and restored his sight.

> *Luke 18:38-42 "And he shouted, saying 'Jesus, Son of David, take pity and have mercy on me!' But those who were in front reproved him, telling him to keep quiet; yet he screamed and shrieked so much the more, 'Son of David, take pity and have mercy on me!' Then Jesus stood still and ordered that he be led to Him; and when he came near, Jesus asked him, 'What do you want Me to do for you?' He said, 'Lord, let me receive my sight!' And Jesus said to Him, 'Receive your sight! (Your trust and confidence that spring from your faith in God) has healed you.'"*

Let your voice be heard in the heavenly realm calling out to Jesus, just like I did the night I was healed. Be determined to get into the Word and press past the hurt and pain. Jesus said, *"Will I find faith in the earth like this?"* This is persistent faith!

It takes persistence in prayer to decide not to give in or give up until we have received what the Lord has promised. That is health and healing to our bodies, hearts and mind as well as our every other need. *We too can stop God and get His attention with determined prayer.* When we give thanks and praise we are saying, "I believe God; I know God will come through." It's not praying without knowing, it's praying with the understanding that the Father will answer and has the answer for all of our needs.

The Prayer of Faith

> **James 5:13-15**
> Is anyone among you afflicted (ill-treated, suffering evil)? He should pray. Is anyone glad at heart? He should sing praise [to God].Is anyone among you sick? He should call in the church elders (the spiritual guides). And they should pray over him, anointing him with oil in the Lord's name. And the prayer [that is] of faith will save him who is sick, and the Lord will restore him; and if he has committed sins, he will be forgiven.

Don't pray in fear but in faith. Jesus hears our cries for help. When we know He has heard us, what we pray and believe we will receive. No form of worry will accomplish anything. Nor will fear. Only faith pleases God and accomplishes healing. To know that you know is the key with no matter of doubt or unbelief in your mind or heart. Doubt will bring no results. Eliminate fear from your mind. Jesus Himself said, 'only believe,' and He is faithful to His word.

Remember also that Jesus himself intercedes for us (Romans 8:26); so does the Holy Spirit. He comes to our aid and bears us up in our weakness;

Stand firm and stand fast in the armour of God.

for we do not know what prayer to offer nor how to offer it worthily as we ought, but the Spirit Himself goes to meet our supplication and pleads on our behalf with unspeakable yearnings and groans too deep for utterance. He prays and intercedes for us in our weakness. He never leaves us nor forsakes us. He is always with us! When we are weak He is strong! We can lean and rely and put our trust and confidence in the Lord Jesus.

> *1 John 5:14*
> *And this is the confidence (the assurance, the privilege of boldness) which we have in Him: [we are sure] that if we ask anything (make any request) according to His will (in agreement with His own plan), He listens to and hears us.*

Standing firm in Prayer and on every occasion Pray at all times.

> *Ephesians 6:14-18 "Stand therefore (hold your ground), having tightened the belt of truth around your loins and having put on the breast plate of integrity and of moral rectitude and right standing with God, and having shod your feet in preparation (to face the enemy with the firm footed stability, the promptness, and the readiness produced by (the good news) of the Gospel of peace.*
>
> *Lift up over all the (covering) shield of saving faith, upon with which you can quench all the flaming missiles of the wicked (one).*
>
> *And take up the helmet of salvation and the sword that the Spirit wields, which is the Word of God.*
>
> *Pray at all times (on every occasion, in every season) in the Spirit, with al l (manner of) prayer and entreaty. To that keep alert and watch with strong purpose and perseverance, interceding in behalf of all the saints (God's consecrated people)."*

Paul the great apostle tells us in 2 Corinthians 12:9 that the Lord's power is made perfect in our weaknesses and infirmities, that the strength and power of Christ may rest upon us. Even when we are weary and weak, He promises to be our strength. His grace is sufficient for us and will never let us Down. Therefore . . . **Never give up!**

The following are the words of a song I wrote during my time of recovery and strength and encouraged me to never give up:

NEVER GIVE UP

He'll make you strong when you are weak.
Give you a song in the midnight hour.
So let your heart sing and be strong, even when the storms are raging, let
it be known, the battle's in His name, He has won.

Never give up, never let go, of the faith you're holding onto. Never give up;
never lose hope in every word that comes from heaven every word He's
spoken . . .
Every breath from heaven, every word He's spoken. He will keep you He
will make you strong.

He'll lift you up in His hands. Carry you on in His strength. So when you've
done all that you can; He'll pick you up to rise with healing in His wings.
You'll live in Him everlasting One.

© Paula Connelly 2005

Be Strong and Courageous

I believe His now word to us is to never give up or lose heart, keep your faith and be strong and courageous for the Lord is with you wherever you go.

We see in Joshua 1:9 the Lord gives these words to Joshua as he was to face new challenges —*'Have I not commanded you, be strong, vigorous and very courageous. Be not afraid, neither be dismayed, for the Lord your God is with you wherever you go'.* When we get into the battles of life, know that the Lord is giving these very words to your heart. Allow them to build your faith and strengthen you to see through and receive your miracle of healing today. The battle is the Lord's and He is with you every step of the way. He is able!

Another great word is in Galatians 6:9: "And do not lose heart and grow weary and faint in acting nobly and doing right for in due time and at the appointed season we shall reap, if we do not loosen and relax our courage and faint."

Again, be encouraged with these words and when you feel as though you are losing heart, **turn to the Word of God and allow His Word to strengthen you** and He will bring to pass all that you have believed for. Even when things don't happen right away as you build your life in the word, you will see the results of Gods promises over time.

The Prayer of Agreement

There are so many aspects of prayer we can learn from, but it's never meant to be complicated. One of them is the prayer of agreement. It's so vital we get into agreement with God's word for our lives. When we line up our lives with His word we are lining them up with His will. It is Gods will, according to His word that we are healed and whole.

Matthew18:19 says, *'Again I tell you, if two of you on earth agree (harmonize together, make a symphony together) about whatever [anything and everything] they may ask, it will come to pass and be done for them by My Father in heaven.'* (And again in other scriptures - John 14:13, Mark 11:22-24.) Believe His word!

Hear these powerful words,' if two of you on earth agree!' There is power in the prayer of agreement with heaven.

Jesus Himself prayed, **'Our father who art in heaven hallowed be thy Name. Thy kingdom come, Thy will be done on earth as it is in heaven.'** Again we are to call the things of heaven into being in this earth.

As we take God at His word and pray according to it, in agreement with two or more, we can know He hears us. This is a wonderful promise.

My prayer is that we may put this into action, see our prayers answered and that many are strengthened and healed as the result.

Finally,
I urge you to hold onto the word of God and to **Never Lose Heart and Never Give up, for God is with you!**

Conclusion

Through our absolute confidence in Jesus Christ and all that He has done on the cross we obtain salvation and healing. As we stand upon the Living Word of God and put it into our hearts, we are transformed and healed from the inside out. It is within the Word we receive our health and healing and the ability to live a prosperous and flourishing life in the fullness of His grace and abundance. As we keep our eyes, our hearts and minds set on the word of God it will bring life. For the word is alive and full of power (Hebrews 4:12).

3 John 2 'Beloved I pray that you may prosper in every way and that your body may keep well, even as I know your soul keeps well and prospers.'

To prosper is to flourish and be strong! God wants us to flourish in our hearts, minds and bodies and every part of our lives.

> *Finally Take the Word as medicine every day ~ For they are life to those that find them, healing and health to all their flesh. (Proverbs 4:22).*

Jesus said these words to remind us everyday He has come to give us life in Abundance and to the fullest measure as we put our trust and hope in Him.

John 10:10
The thief comes only in order to steal and kill and destroy. I came that they may have and enjoy life, and have it in abundance (to the full, till it overflows).

Prayer to invite Jesus into your heart:

Dear Jesus,

I come to you and invite you into my heart. Forgive me of my sins, heal my heart and make me whole from the inside out. I give you all my past, hurts, disappointments and fears, I ask you Jesus to come into my heart and make me a new person from the inside out. Give me your strength to live each day as I put my trust in you.

Amen.

Prayer for Healing:

Dear Lord Jesus,

I need you in my life, help me to live in and through You. I put my trust in Your Word to bring healing and health to my heart, my mind and my body. Renew and strengthen me today on the inside. Thank you Lord Jesus for healing me and giving me a new heart!

Amen.

More Scriptures to Encourage You:

Proverbs 4:23 "Keep and guard your heart with all vigilance and above all that you guard, for out of it flow the springs of life."

Isaiah 55:8 "For My thoughts are not your thoughts, neither are your ways My ways, says the Lord, for as the heavens are higher than the earth so are My ways higher than your ways and My thoughts than your thoughts."

John 14: Jesus says "Do not let your hearts be troubled, (distressed, agitated)."

Proverbs 4:20-21 "My Son, attend to my words, consent and submit to my sayings. Let them not depart from your sight; keep them in the centre of your heart."

1 Peter 5:7 "Casting the whole of your care (all your anxieties, all your worries, all your concerns once and for all) on Him, for He cares for you affectionately and cares about you watchfully.'

Psalm 91 "He who dwells in the secret place of the Most High shall remain stable and fixed under the shadow of the Almighty (whose power no foe can withstand). I will say of the Lord He is my refuge and my fortress, my God; on Him I lean and rely and in Him I (confidently) trust!"

Ephesians 4:22-24 "Strip yourselves of your former nature (put off and discard your old un-renewed self) which characterized your previous manner of life and becomes corrupt through lusts and desires that spring form delusion; and constantly renewed in the spirit of your mind (having a fresh mental and spiritual attitude) and put on the new nature (the regenerate self) created in God's image (Godlike) in true righteousness and holiness."

Proverbs 4:24 "Put far from you false and dishonest speech and wilful and contrary talk put far from you."

Proverbs 13:3 "He who guards his mouth keeps his life, but he who opens wide his lips comes to ruin."

Romans 10: 8, 9 "But what does it say? The Word (Gods message in Christ) is near you, on your lips and in your heart; that is the Word of faith which we preach, because if you acknowledge and confess with your lips that Jesus is Lord and in your heart believe (adhere to trust in and rely on the truth) that God raised Him from the dead, you will be saved.'

Philippians 4:6 "Do not fret or have any anxiety about anything but in every circumstance and in everything by prayer and petition with thanksgiving, continue to make your wants known to God. And God's peace shall be yours that tranquil state of a soul assured of its salvation through Christ, and so fearing nothing from God and being content with its earthly lot of whatever sort that is, that peace) which transcends all understanding shall garrison and mount guard over your hearts and minds in Christ Jesus."

1 John 4:18 "There is no fear in love (dread does not exist), but full grown (complete, perfect) love turns fear out of doors and expels every trace of terror! For fear brings with it the thought of punishment and so he who is afraid has not reached the full maturity of love (is not yet grown into loves complete perfection)."

2 Timothy 1:7 "For God did not give us a spirit of timidity (of cowardice, of craven and cringing and fawning fear), but (He has given us a spirit) of power and of love and of calm and well balanced mind and discipline and self control."

Colossians 3:2 "And set your minds and keep them set on what is above (the higher things), not on the things that are on earth."

Hebrews 13: 5b "For God Himself has said, I will not in any way fail you, nor give you up, nor leave you without support. I will not, I will not, I will not in any degree leave you helpless nor forsake nor let you down (relax my hold on you)! (Assuredly not!)"

John 14:12-13

I assure you, most solemnly I tell you, if anyone steadfastly believes in Me, he will himself be able to do the things that I do; and he will do even greater things than these, because I go to the Father.

[13]And I will do [I Myself will grant] whatever you ask in My Name [as presenting all that I AM], so that the Father may be glorified and extolled in (through) the Son.

Mark 11:23-24

Truly I tell you, whoever says to this mountain, Be lifted up and thrown into the sea! And does not doubt at all in his heart but believes that what he says will take place, it will be done for him.

[24]For this reason I am telling you, whatever you ask for in prayer, believe (trust and be confident) that it is granted to you, and you will [get it].

OTHER PRODUCTS AND RESOURES AVAILABLE

To Contact the writer contact:
Email: paula@paulaconnelly.com
Website www.paulaconnelly.com

Worship Albums available by Paula Connelly:

'Just Believe'—solo Album songs of hope and faith.

'Inside Out'—Instrumental Worship. Includes the single of 'Inside out'—sung by Paula